MW00440374

Advance Praise for *Letters from Planet Corona*

Many have turned to me asking, "Why the plague!" In my first zoom lecture after Pesach, I spoke about "Why Corona?" Now, I have an insightful volume which I can recommend to my students. Your collection of letters, which you wrote regarding the reality of "Planet Corona," is a poetic and literary gem.

You have given us a worthwhile present to comprehend our present situation. With all the sadness in the current reality, you stress our accomplishments—food, clothing, shelter, and survival during this period. You enhance your perspective with your many citations from Rabbinic and general literature. You utilize Jewish history to place the present crisis within its context.

I highly recommend your composition to all who seek guidance and solace. May the Almighty soon terminate "Planet Corona" and may we happily return to terra firma.

Chizki V' Imtzi,
Aaron Rakeffet

Rabbi and professor of Rabbinic Literature at Yeshiva University's Gruss Institute in Jerusalem. Noted scholar, author, and teacher. Author of many articles and books, among them:

Bernard Revel: Builder of American Jewish Orthodox
From Washington Avenue to Washington Street

For better or for worse, our world changed dramatically during 2020. A gruesome pandemic, world-wide lockdowns, the separation of families, the heartbreaking phenomenon of people dying alone without loved ones to support them. Deviation from "normal" became the "new normal." Even those of us who were at little risk had a deep sense of unease, confusion, and uncertainty.

Like most of us, Chaya Passow was one of those people. But she took her fears, anxieties, insecurities, and confusion and channeled them into something constructive and liberating. Over the first seven months, she compiled 70 letters from Planet Corona, a wild, wacky and sometimes ominous and scary place bearing only some resemblance to our familiar planet Earth.

These letters are not Pollyannish or saccharine. Chaya Passow is very open and honest about the very real fears and frustrations that she, and we, experienced but she brings humor, hope, and optimism to a difficult situation—reminding us all that a change in attitude can change the realities.

Shining with precious lessons of emunah—faith in a loving God who will sustain us and nurture us even when we are helpless and vulnerable, and faith in ourselves—Chaya Passow's optimism and resilience as expressed in these letters are truly contagious. And this type of contagion can only be positive!

With admiration and bracha,
Yitzchak A. Breitowitz
Rav, Kehillas Ohr Somayach, Jerusalem
Professor Emeritus, University of Maryland Law School

Letters from Planet Corona

Chaya Passow

Letters from Planet Corona

City of Gold Press
planetcorona18@gmail.com
www.lettersfromplanetcorona.com

Copyright © Chaya M. Passow, 2020

All rights reserved. No part of this publication may be
reproduced, stored in a retrieval system, or transmitted in any form
or by any means, electronic, mechanical, photocopying or otherwise,
without the prior permission of the publisher, except in the case
of brief quotations embodied in critical articles or reviews.

ISBN 978-965-599-405-6, paperback

Printed and bound in Israel.

Dedicated to

My dear husband, Eli.
You are truly
"The wind beneath my wings."

And to our dear children and grandchildren:
Akiva and Hinda Fuld – Tzofia, Michael Avichai, Chana,
Elyakim, Chedva, Elchanan, and Tova
Yitzchak and Adina Groyer – Rifael, Zahava, Teela, Meir,
Esti, Chani, and Yoel Avrohom
David Hoffman and Shuli Passow – Idan and Azriel
Avigdor and Malvina Fuld – Oriel, Talia, and Shirel
Simcha and Hindy Fuld – Michoel Aharon, Tzipporah, Yosef
Chaim, Yisroel Meir, Malky, Batsheva, Yonah, and Yehuda
Nati and Rachel KatzPassow – Zamir and Niso
Mordechai and Aliza Burg – Bracha, Chana, Racheli, Shira,
Miriam, and Michoel Shlomo
Dani Passow
Eliezer and Chana Fuld – Michoel Yehuda, Liba, Tali,
Shayna, Ayala, and Rina

Contents

Prologue

I never started out to write a book. It would never have entered my mind. Since early childhood, I've been a bibliophile. Even more, I've almost worshipped books. I read voraciously. And I certainly would never have considered defacing a book in any way. Blasphemy.

Authors were near-mythic characters who could create these wonderful gifts that occupied, entertained, even mesmerized me for hours on end. People like me read books, enjoyed them, could be engrossed in them. However, we didn't *write* them.

Then one day in March, shortly after the holiday of Purim, I looked out my Jerusalem window and beheld a strange new world. No one was on the streets. There were no sounds of traffic. We heard that schools, restaurants, theaters, stores, nearly everything, were closed or closing. We knew of people who were sick. And then, a close friend died of Covid-19 shortly before Passover.

Where was I? I didn't recognize my beloved city, country, or world anymore. I felt so terribly disoriented and I wrote a letter from the new and alien world in which I was presently living. I named it Planet Corona and shared it with a few friends via e-mail.

Somehow, the letters kept coming. I wasn't even sure from where they emerged. What had begun as a way of reassuring myself, forming my thoughts, even taming my demons, became an outpouring that soothed, enriched, and quite surprised me. And, apparently, my letters connected to similar needs in those with whom I was sharing the letters. There were encouraging responses and, after a while, suggestions that they be published.

Perhaps the reaction that I cherished most, was that readers felt as though I were speaking to them personally. They heard my voice and shared in a mutual perspective. That is what I wished to achieve. I hope I have been successful.

I am grateful to my friends and family who responded to my letters and offered comments and encouragement. So, thanks to Adina, Aliza, Ayelet, Chana F, Chana S, Chaya G, Chaya W, Danielle, Deena, Diane, Emilie, Georgina, Joan, Julie, Nechama, Rachel, Reena, Shellie, Toby, Tzilia, and Yael.

A special thanks to my very good friend and editor, Shirley Zauer, whose professionalism and friendship managed to go hand-in-hand during the editing process. Shirley honored my desire to allow for a conversational style and edited with an exacting but gentle hand.

Thanks also to my "shepherd" and publicist, Stuart Schnee, for his indefatigable efforts at all stages of this book.

Words are inadequate to express my love and gratitude for two very special women who've been supportive and encouraging, not only in the process of the production of this book but also in helping keep me sane during this period and, indeed, for decades. However, words are what I *have*, and so I want to thank my sister Rivka Wolitzky and dear friend Dvora Kidorf just for being there.

There would have been no book at all were it not for my dear husband, Eli, who has encouraged and supported me during every step of this endeavor. He has been there throughout, cheering me on, offering astute advice, and been a true partner in every way. I am truly fortunate.

If we've learned anything from this pandemic, it's that there is no one to depend on other than Hashem. *Ein od Milvado.* "There is *no one* other than Him." In the process of writing these letters, I've almost felt as though I were somehow channeling ideas, thoughts, and words. Who knows? I *do* know that I have never felt more dependent upon, but also never as close to Him as now. For that I am most grateful.

Welcome to Planet Corona.

Chapter One

March 2020

March 17, 2020

We Land on the Planet

First, a disclaimer. I've never considered myself much of a writer. I like to speak and teach, but I never write out my shiurim or talks since I'm comfortable speaking extemporaneously. However, right now my (our) access to live teaching and discussing is severely hampered, so I am turning to writing. Maybe an "upside" of all this (obviously a minor one considering everything) will be to uncover some literary ability hidden within. Or maybe not. But I've had a lot of thoughts about our present crisis and feel that I want to share them.

I'm going to try to keep these "letters" reasonably short, although I've been kind of overwhelmed with thoughts and ideas and my attempts to make some sense of all of this. However, I won't cover everything in any one "letter." Obviously, I can't. So I'll just start. Right now.

First, let me explain "Planet Corona" or, at least, why I use that phrase. I have been feeling extremely bewildered for a while now. As if the whole world is different, confusing, and frankly, frighteningly unrecognizable. Like a different planet that I happened to land on. But now I'm thinking that we've always lived on Planet Corona. It's just that now, we know it.

Someone said to me recently that she was just waiting for this to happen. With world travel so common and with the potential of infections still very much with us, it was clear to her that at some point something would spread quickly and, perhaps, uncontrollably. Maybe you've seen the *Ted Talks* with Bill Gates predicting just such a catastrophe in 2015 or the uncanny passages from a Dean Koontz book called *The Eyes of Darkness* published in 1981.

However, what I believe the coronavirus has stripped away are many of our illusions. Illusions that we are in control, that science and medicine are so advanced that they somehow can deal with anything. Societal illusions about the inviolability and limitlessness of our individual desires and aspirations. And, perhaps, some understanding that although we have voluntarily isolated ourselves from others by our incessant involvement with our hand-held technology and "virtual friends," we are, in fact, more interconnected than we realize and we very much *need* real, tangible friends and family who don't need to stay 2 meters away, or even further.

Hashem* has made Himself abundantly clear! His protection of us, that is. Our planet, Earth, is always jam-packed with bacteria, viruses, and pathogens that could conceivably kill us. We are miraculously protected from them the vast majority of the time. Were we not to be, THIS is what could and would happen.

We know the midrash quoted by Rashi in Parshat Beshalach (Exodus 17:8). After the People of Israel experienced all the miracles of the Exodus from Egypt, the Splitting of the Red Sea, and God's providing them with water and with manna, they have the audacity to ask, "Is Hashem in our midst or not?" Immediately following that challenge come the words "…and Amalek came."

Rashi asks what the connection is between these two verses. He writes:

> The Torah juxtaposed this passage with the preceding verse to say, "I am always among you and ready for all of your needs, yet you say, 'Is Hashem in our midst or not?' By your lives, the

2

dog (Amalek) will bite you. And you will shout to Me and know where I am." This is compared to a man who placed his son on his shoulder and set out on a journey. That son saw an object and said, "Father, take that object and give it to me." He gave it to him. And so, too, a second time and so, too, a third. They encountered a man. The son said to the man, "Have you seen Father?" His father said to him, "Do you not know where I am?" He cast him down from upon his shoulder and the dog came and bit him.

We are always riding on God's shoulders. Only now, on Planet Corona, we are getting a vivid idea, dramatically presented, of what Earth looks like when it becomes Planet Corona. And, I would venture to say, that might well be a very good thing.

* A Hebrew name for God.

March 19, 2020

Little Things Mean a Lot

(And what's interesting is that I was never so aware that I actually am on a *planet*, along with *all humanity*)

Do you remember *Horton Hears a Who*? Well, briefly, it's a book by the inimitable Dr. Seuss about Horton the elephant that discovers that there's a microscopic civilization called Whoville, populated by Whos, existing on the tip of a thistle and he finds that he has to protect them from forces that would destroy Whoville because they don't believe it exists. The refrain/message of the book is "A person is a person, no matter how small."

I thought about this book as I've set about exploring Planet Corona. (Of course, it's rather a virtual expedition, taking place within the walls of my apartment and in my head.) One characteristic of Planet Corona is the emphasis on things small, even microscopically so. Of course, we begin with the very tiny virus that is bringing the world to its knees; that representative of the micro-world that has always been with us, but which we rarely notice until it affects (or infects) us. Quite a bit larger, but still on a smallish scale, are the young grandchildren who, I am told, are little "virus spreaders" now posing a threat to the grandparents who love and miss them!

But then we have some of the small things that are making this experience much more bearable, such as the myriads of pixels that make up the images on my Smart Phone sent to me by friends and family with funny videos, inspirational messages, photos of family, etc. Not to mention the dear faces of family and friends on Skype and WhatsApp that allow me to conduct "safe visits." Of course, I couldn't enjoy any of these without the huge numbers of tiny cones and rods in my eyes that allow me to see these images. In color. Thank you, God.

Other "small things" on Planet Corona are the flowers outside my window whose colors glow with the rain and, sometimes, with the sun upon them. And my tiny taste buds that allow me to enjoy the good food that I still have in my home and is still available in the stores. There are the tiny soap bubbles that appear to rid my hands of potential coronavirus contamination. As long as I wash properly. Which, my husband is delighted to note, I have begun to do. And I've not even scratched the surface.

On Planet Corona, there's even a focus on Nothings, or rather No Things, as Rabbi David Aaron calls those very real but invisible "things" that make life not only bearable, but also meaningful and even transcendent, such as Love, Friendship, Wisdom, Trust, Caring, etc. And, of course, chief among these is God and our relationship with Him, which can be experienced in the smallest of small as well as the largest of large.

I had a glimpse of Planet Corona before I actually got here when I visited the Bird Sanctuary outside Eilat a few weeks ago. We learned many amazing facts about birds and bird migrations so relevant here in Israel, which is perhaps the most important corridor, at least in the Eastern hemisphere, for birds migrating from Europe and parts of Asia to Africa.

But the "small" item that grabbed my attention, and filled me with wonder (and gratitude), was the tiny, 6-gram bird that flies from Finland each year to southern Africa. The parent birds leave before the fledglings, and so the question is, how do these tiny creatures know how and where to fly with no parents to guide them?

The answer, given by the ornithologist-in-training, is that they read the stars in the night sky! That means they navigate using the ever-changing star formations in the skies overhead from Finland to Africa! And they never even went to astronomy school. They also can "see" the Earth's magnetic fields which help them navigate north to south! We have obviously underestimated the "bird brain."

We live in an astonishingly complex, absorbingly fascinating world both in the macrocosm and, perhaps even more amazing, in the microcosm. A gift from God just for "little old me," an atomic particle-sized dot in the cosmos. *Bishvili nivra ha'olam* (the world was created for me).

The view from Planet Corona can be quite breathtaking.

March 20, 2020

Faces

One thing about Planet Corona is that faces here are so much more important! You learn to crave and savor faces other than your own, even in a picture or on a video chat. The smiling faces of grand-children so proud of the beautiful art creation they made in their "spare time." The face of my *chavruta** as we continue our learning of Sefer Devarim (Deuteronomy) on Skype. The faces of the people in the local supermarket on my brief trips there, my hands clad in plastic gloves and being sure to maintain a *"daled amot,"* aka a 2-meter distance.

A face, whose orifices are also the means of transmitting the coronavirus, is also that which makes us unique. God has passed his Oneness on to us in the way that not one human face, since the beginning of time, has been exactly like any other. Our faces, with their orifices, speak, hear, see, smell. Faces are the way we present ourselves to and communicate with others. Eyes are truly the "windows of the soul."

Our mouths allow us to speak with human speech—creative, imaginative, abstract, emotional—and that distinguishes us from the rest of Creation. Smells are evocative, and hearing—or, better, listening—is at least half of conversing. Our faces as a whole communicate feelings and reflect often more than we are aware of.

Our faces are both revelatory and potent. Anything that is done or communicated face-to-face is most open, direct, powerful, compassionate, loving (or the opposite, as in "in your face!"). It is also where intimacy often occurs. That is why the highest accolade of Moshe at the end of his days is that he spoke with God "face-to-face," which is the highest level of prophecy and closeness to God and His purpose.

Frankly, I miss the faces of my life. Even the faces of strangers that I get to glimpse rarely, seem more radiant than they ever did before. I long to kiss the faces of my loved ones. Or even just gaze into their eyes from close up. The face of my mother, a"h, was probably the very first image, the very first entity, that was meaningful and special to me. It was a long time ago. I've never lost my taste for faces.

Here on Planet Corona, each face is a unique treasure and pleasure.

* Learning partner.

March 22, 2020

Hands

Have you noticed that on Planet Corona hands are unusually… noticeable? It's not that they're outsized, like the hands in a Rodin sculpture. And they don't actually glow to attract attention. But they are disproportionately prominent. They can be threatening, so they must be washed frequently and properly (20 seconds, which is the time it takes to sing "Happy Birthday to You" twice!) and they must be gloved when you are outside.

Today, shopping for groceries, the owner handed me plastic gloves as I entered the store. I feel like either a physician or a cleaning lady. And we can't shake hands, hug one another, kiss either the mezuza or the Torah, and it's essentially "hands off" for now.

Of course, it's not something we haven't come across before. Hands have always had sinister potential. Fists punch, hands slap and make threatening or even vulgar motions. Even metaphorically there are negative "handy" phrases. One can be tight-fisted, or arrive empty-handed. Events can get out-of-hand (like the coronavirus epidemic, perhaps?) and one can "lose money hand over fist" (and isn't that apropos right now?).

However, we need to keep in mind that "hand" conjures up many more positive associations and metaphors. Hands caress, heal, comfort, share, clasp affectionately, and much more. Juliet says, "And palm to palm is holy palmers' kiss." *Tzedaka*, charity, goes from hand to hand and bonds giver to receiver. Hands knead challah, prepare food, knit warm hats for grandchildren and soldiers, and type "Letters From Planet Corona" to reach out to others.

Metaphorically, too, much that is positive is associated with hands. One may be open-handed and even-handed. We can "give a hand" either by helping out someone or applauding their achievements. We can be someone's "right hand wo/man," allowing another to depend on us. In the Beit Hamikdash (the Temple), the Kohen cleansed his hands before beginning his duties to consecrate them to the service of Hashem. That is something we emulate each morning as we begin our morning and our *tefillot* (prayers), when we wash and say the blessing "*Al netilat yadayim*" to symbolically ready our own hands as they serve Hashem and perform *mitzvot* (commandments) during our day.

Hands are the instruments of action and of honest labor. In Genesis 33:3, Jacob gives his son Joseph a unique coat of *passim*, a descriptive word with various possible interpretations. One meaning derives from the Aramaic word for "palm," suggesting that the overlong coat sleeves covered the palm of Joseph's hand. That would explain what angered his brothers—because someone with such long sleeves can't work. He'd get dirty. This was a further example of Joseph being spoiled by his father and receiving special favor.

So, today on Planet Corona, we wash our hands and keep them out of our eyes and mouth and cover them with latex when we venture forth. We miss the days when we could caress and hug our grandchildren, shake hands with friends, hold hands and dance at a wedding, or comfort a friend with a pat on the shoulder. We yearn for those days to return.

But, in the meantime, we can still do many of the things that hands do and do so well and we can and should thank Hashem for these amazing creations, the most complex in our entire skeletal structure. (The hands contain more than a quarter of the bones in the entire body.)

And we can hug ourselves both figuratively and emotionally. We can "reach out" to Hashem and to our friends through the means that are acceptable. And, perhaps, we can "hand over" to Hashem all of our delusions of control along with our worries and fears. Let's give a hand to hands.

March 23, 2020

A Disclaimer

If you have read any or all of my previous "letters," I'm afraid that I may have come across as somewhat "Pollyanna"ish. (If you don't know who she is, you now have time to Google her and find out!). I am not at all so enamored of this Planet that I never want to return to Planet Earth, though I sincerely hope to take some of Planet Corona back with me.

I recognize that many are experiencing extremely difficult challenges here such as loss of income, painful loneliness, depression, increased family violence exacerbated by prolonged contact in close quarters, etc. I think we must all pray for people in such harsh circumstances and help whenever possible with communications, *tzedaka*, and, in short, in any way we can.

What I have been trying to do and will continue to attempt to do is to glean from this unprecedented experience any lessons for better understanding the human condition, for self-improvement, for a closer connection to Hashem and to others. I feel that this is too powerful a wake-up call not to try to learn and grow from this experience so that when we do return to Planet Earth (may it be soon)—the wonderful and amazing place that Hashem created and gave to us with His Love—we will take the learning and growth and make Earth a much better place than it was before we were transported to Planet Corona.

March 23, 2020

The Gift of the Present

When you get to Planet Corona, the first thing they do is give you a gift (isn't that just lovely?). Actually, they call it "a present." In fact, that's just what it is, the Present. Now. And you begin to learn what an exceptionally generous gift it is. Perhaps, the best one you or anyone else has ever received. Because, here on Planet Corona, no one (and I mean *no one*) seems to really know how we got here and arrived at this exact position.

So, we have no past, at least none that we can make anything of. And no one (and I *really* mean *no one*) has any idea where we are going from here. So, we don't seem to have a future, either. At least not one we can anticipate. In place of the Past, we have conjectures and theories with little agreement. As for the Future, it's mostly at the crystal ball stage.

So what we have is *now*. Only, that's all you have ever had. The past, whatever happened, is over and done with. The future isn't here yet. We're left with this moment, whomever we're with, wherever we are, whatever we're doing. However, most of us are unused to living that way.

We constantly dwell on and live in the past, sometimes with pleasure, more often with painful feelings of guilt, remorse, or regret. We look to the future, sometimes in eager anticipation, but frequently with worry and trepidation.

The negative emotions usually outnumber the positive ones, but they both detract from our presence in the present with the people, places, and activities of the Here and Now. Studies have shown that most people spend 50 percent of their conscious time on thoughts of the past or the future. It's been demonstrated that doing so detracts from one's happiness. Surprisingly, it's been found that even those who dwell on pleasant thoughts of the past or future are happier when they focus on the present.

Many years ago, when I was 14 (OK, many, many years ago!), I heard Carol Burnett sing a song called "Meantime." It made such an impression on me that I remember most of the lyrics to this day, even though I haven't heard it since then. That is, until a few hours ago when I searched for it on YouTube to check if I remembered the lyrics correctly. The theme of the song is that much happened "Before I was born" and much will happen "After I'm gone."

And those are events that I wasn't and won't be a part of. So, what's left for me is "the meantime," i.e., my lifetime.

But I would go even further. All I really have is *this moment* to do all my living, all that I can do right now. That's it. To truly be with the people I'm with at the moment, giving full attention to what I'm saying, listening to, or doing. They say that Henny Machlis, z"l,* had that ability, to focus totally on whomever she was with and on whatever they were saying. Now *that* is a gift. A "present" if you will.

The story is told of a rabbi walking to the study hall who was stopped by a town guard and challenged with, "Where are you going?" The rabbi answered, "I don't know." He was asked again, angrily, and he returned the same answer. The guard had him arrested and each day, as he sat in jail he was asked, "Tell us where you were going." And each time he answered, "I don't know." Finally, the head judge had him brought forth and asked, "Why are you continuing in your stubbornness? Tell us where you were going and you can be released." The rabbi said, "But I told the truth. I *intended* to go to the study hall, but you see, I ended up in jail. So in fact, I didn't know where I was going!"

So, it's true that I really have no idea how I got here. And, I haven't the foggiest notion where I'm going or when. None of us does. Therefore, we might as well live fully in the present, in the surroundings, situation, and with the people of here and now. It's all we have and, frankly, it's quite a lot.

* A true *eishet chayil* who provided sustenance of all kinds to dozens of guests from all walks of life every single Shabbat in her modest home in Jerusalem.

March 24, 2020

Traveling and Staying Put

There are a few items that are easy to find on Planet Corona (unlike toilet paper), and they are going cheap. Such as devices with Waze, GPS or GoogleMaps, compasses, and other navigation aids. They're totally useless. People can't even give them away. Kind of like your old VCR 8-track tapes or my husband's vast collection of classical music LPs in mint condition. Of course they're useless because… well, where are you going, after all?

There is a sense of relief in not hearing the robotic voice that tells you "At the roundabout… continue straight." Do I really need to be told *not* to change direction? Although on my own and now useless Waze program, my granddaughter Esti dubbed instructions in her own voice. So now I take back-seat driving instructions from a rather bossy 12-year-old! Although, she's inevitably right and, truthfully, I prefer her voice to Amy's. And besides, her "back-seat" is 6,000 miles away in Far Rockaway and I miss her.

But, for right now, most of us don't need any navigational aids because we're not going far. Or, for that matter, even near. And for so many of us, this is a big change. I was actually a late-comer to the use of Waze, but I had grown very dependent on it even when traveling to familiar places just in case there were construction or traffic delays of which I wasn't aware. But I haven't heard that bossy voice in weeks, one of the indications that, for the most part, we are all staying put.

Yet, for the last few decades we've taken advantage of the shrinking globe and traveled far and near. When you perused any Shabbat magazine, the vast majority of ads were for travel to everywhere in the world you could imagine and others you probably hadn't heard of. Israelis travel the globe. "What, you haven't been to Lapland yet?!" "We're taking the cruise to Antarctica next month when we return from the cruise to Alaska." And this is not an exaggeration.

And, we haven't yet touched on all the places you could go, outside of Eretz Yisrael, of course, for Pesach. The list is endless. Only, on Planet Corona this has come to a grinding halt. Nothing. Nada. Nearly all families will most likely be spending the Seder around the family table with their nuclear family. Sort of the way it used to be on Earth before it all went crazy.

Why have we been running around so much? Not only traveling, but shopping, "doing lunch" (mea culpa), even running from one shiur or program to another. Just to go "somewhere else." What have we been seeking? Happiness? It seems we're not happier as a result. Self-fulfillment? Well, have we felt fulfilled? Physical pleasure? But we all know that that is an endless and ever-deepening pit. The Midrash warns us, "No man leaves this world with even half the material acquisitions he desired."

One of Hashem's "names" is *Hamakom*. In fact, on Seder night we will recite the words "*Baruch Hamakon, baruch hu*" "Blessed is the Makom, blessed is he." In Midrash Kohelet, it says: "Why is Hashem called "Makom?" For He is the "makom" (location) of the Universe, but the Universe is not His "makom."

Just two weeks ago (it seems like years!) we read in Megillat Esther that Mordechai admonished Esther, saying that if she did not go to help the Jews, then help and salvation would come from another Makom, which is a veiled reference to Hashem. Hashem *is* Makom, place, location. And, we have a spark of Hashem within us. Which I think suggests that we have the essence of "makom" inside us, too.

And if you are already in the right place or if the right place is in you, then where are you rushing off to? You're already there. Everything you need is within you. And now you have a chance to look within for your happiness, self-fulfillment, sense of worth, and indeed, for pleasure. The pleasure of being grounded instead of frenetic.

Here on Planet Corona you have been given a great opportunity. To get to know yourself. To know that you don't need to go out of yourself to find yourself. Dorothy in *The Wizard of Oz* sings "Somewhere over the Rainbow" at the beginning of the movie. But by the end she clicks her ruby slippers and says, "There's no place like home."

Home is wherever you are because it is within each and every one of us. Hashem asked that the Jewish people build a Mishkan [tabernacle] "to dwell within them," i.e., within us. If the Makom wished to dwell within us, then "within" is the only destination of real worth.

"Return again, return again, return to the land of your soul. Return to who you are, return to what you are, return to where you are born and reborn again" (Rabbi Shlomo Carlebach).

Happy and safe travels!

March 25, 2020

Aging 'Baby-boomers'

One thing that isn't so very different on Planet Corona is the planet's focus on *me*! Well, I don't mean me personally, but rather the population cohort in which I find myself. You know, the Golden Agers, retirees, elderly (if you must), but more specifically, my own sub-division, the Baby Boomers. We are the ones (born 1944–1964) who have held center stage essentially from the time we were born. We were the "miracle children" born after WWII and perhaps more significantly for Jews, after the Holocaust, who were pampered and spoiled and cherished.

We subsequently turned on our indulgent parents and told them we knew everything better and that you couldn't really trust anyone over 30! We became the hippies and flower-children of the 60s, marching for causes such as the Vietnam War and Soviet Jewry, amongst many others. We then became the "me" generation (which, arguably, we always had been and have been ever since).

As we got older, the focus was on our "mid-life crises," and ultimately on what to do during retirement. It's not just that that was *our* focus, it appeared to have been everyone's, largely because studies show that we Boomers are the largest consumers of widespread media and they tell us what we want to hear. Have you noticed that ever since our co-Boomers in the acting field have aged, so have the central roles in major films?

So, it's not so surprising that we are, once again, the focus of attention on Planet Corona. Everyone is worrying about us since we are the most vulnerable population to contract the virus with much more serious consequences. But rather than feeling smug, somewhat self-centered, or perhaps self-conscious, I think we may be feeling, as strange as it might sound, *cherished*.

The younger generations are being inconvenienced, to put it very mildly, essentially to keep us from getting ill or dying. It's true that it is painful for many of us to be separated from children and, even more importantly, grandchildren, but we are all cognizant of the fact that they are staying away to protect us. Especially when, under normal circumstances, our kids would be ringing our phones off the hook to ask us for baby-sitting services.

It's very sweet actually, and reflects the reverence that Jewish tradition has always had for its older members. Anyone, of any age, who is wise and worthy of respect is called a "*zakein* [elder]." Even our buses have always carried a sign saying "*mipnei sayva takum*" "stand before an older person" on the first reserved seats at the front of the bus. Grandparents and other older people are generally given places of honor at family gatherings and on other occasions.

This is not something we should take for granted. A friend who is in Leipzig, Germany for a few weeks conducting research for her doctorate and is now caught there due to the crisis wrote to me that she had to go shopping for groceries a few days ago. The store only allowed a small number to enter at a time and so the line was very long and the temperature stood at 40° F. In the line were elderly people with walkers and canes and no one allowed them to go ahead in the line.

My friend tried to allow older people to get ahead of her, but had to stop because of the angry remarks from the other shoppers. She ended up giving her own place to older people and doing that repeatedly as she worked her way backward. Unfortunately, she never made it into the store. However, she told each older person or couple, "I have to give you my place and help you because I'm Jewish."

What's the difference here on Planet Corona from the way it was before? I think that the emphasis previously was, at least partly, on how useful we were. Personally, I ran an unofficial taxi service, gave English lessons, baby-sat, etc. Don't misunderstand. Often, we actually enjoy helping out and being useful. Perhaps it makes us feel *young!* A Baby Boomer's dream. It's also true that, for the most part, our relationships are founded on love and respect.

However, it's also true that we have been expected to run "*Kaytanot Savta,*"* have families over for Shabbat and chagim even when it isn't *quite* convenient, and be the "on call" babysitter in a crunch, or even on a regular basis. And we've loved it. Mostly. Only now, we can't do any of those things. We're not as "useful" as we've been in the past. We just *are.*

Nevertheless, we are being cherished and protected because we are loved, respected, and vulnerable. Because if we ever do hope to have a promising future, it will have to be built on the best of the past. And we Boomers are the repositories of that past. And on Planet Corona, everyone seems to realize that. We do too.

* Grandma's day care center.

March 27, 2020

?

The most utilized punctuation mark on Planet Corona is not the period. Periods are too definite as in, "No, you cannot have another piece of cake. Period." It's not an exclamation point because, well life is exciting enough as it is. We could probably use a little less turmoil and turbulence. No, the most popular punctuation mark is the question mark.

Not because it is overused by teenage girls as in "I'll see ya' in 10 minutes at the mall, okay?" but due to the fact that we are surrounded by questions with precious few answers. "How am I going to make Pesach with bored children in the house 24/7?" "Will I get arrested if I walk an extra 10 meters from my home?" "Can I do Pesach shopping outside of my neighborhood?" Or, perhaps, "Why did this happen?" or "If Hashem is sending a message, what is it?"

Yet the unassailable truth is that unanswerable questions have always lurked at the back of our private and national minds. Children proverbially ask, "Why is the sky blue?" or "Why can't I stay outside longer?" But also, "Why did Zayde go to *Shamayim* [Heaven]?" And grown-ups want to know and understand, "Why did I lose my job just as my daughter is about to be married" or just generally, "Why is this happening to me?"

So we give or search for answers, simple ones or more complex ones, depending on the complexity of the questions. Because we are uncomfortable with uncertainty. And sometimes the answers we give are unsatisfying to the questioner, and sometimes we feel we must provide *some* answer, correct or not, because we can't just leave that question hanging in the air, admitting that we don't know the answer, that maybe we don't have a clue.

And there are the national theological questions such as the one Gideon asks the angel in Judges 6:13, "I beg you my lord, if Hashem is with us, why has all this befallen us?" or as Esther is said to have asked in Psalms 22, "My God, my God, why have You forsaken me?" as she ventures forth to save her people. And perhaps the most problematical question, the one that Moses himself was unable to answer, "Why do bad things happen to good people and good things to evil ones?", the question that forms the basis for the philosophical quandary called theodicy. But we seek almost obsessively for answers, anything to assuage the confusion and discomfort of not having an answer.

Science claims that it has answers. "Why is the sky blue, Abba?" "Well, let me tell you, dear son, what I read in a scientific book." Except that science can tell us *how* things work, can teach about cause and effect in physics, can explain the inner workings of much natural phenomena. But it falls short on the big questions of "Why," those which indicate our search for meaning and understanding. And we so desperately want to understand what often seems like a disordered and chaotic world.

However, here on Planet Corona we've learned what is taught in our traditional texts, "Divine blessing only rests on that which is hidden from the eye" (Bava Metzia 42a). That which is weighed, measured, or counted is too definite, too bounded to allow for blessed expansion, for the often unexpected bounty which exists in potential, but not where boundaries have already been firmly established. And that's where the beauty of questions enters the picture.

Until a question is answered, there are perhaps countless possible answers, including ones that we haven't even imagined. While it's true that the resolution of quandaries brings a sense of relief, it also can kill hope. Sometimes, uncertainty can be an acceptable price to pay for blessings and wonder and hopeful prayer.

Our commentaries tell us that on his death bed Jacob wished to reveal the future to his sons, but his *ruach hakodesh** left him so that he was unable to do so. It appears that he wished to tell them that their sojourn in Egypt was not to be forever and that they would one day reach the Holy Land, and that it would all end with the coming of the Messiah. But, clearly, Hashem had other plans. Perhaps, because, as comforting as it would be to know that in a certain year the People of Israel would assuredly leave Egypt, they would also have to know that until that time they would *not* leave.

And even had Jacob been able to foretell and share with his sons when the Messiah would come to bring all of mankind to its final days of blessing and peace, we would also have been heavily burdened knowing that it wouldn't happen until then. The question of "When will the Messiah finally arrive?" is still preferable to the knowledge that he is certainly not coming at this particular painful time. Killing hope is a death blow to a life.

So we live with the question mark on Planet Corona. No one seems to have answers to "How long?" "How do we manage?" "What should we best do in the meantime?" and certainly not to "Why did this happen?" But without answers we do not limit our relationships, our creativity, our growth and our *emuna* (faith) in Hashem. We leave our possibilities open, and nearly infinite. We don't limit our potential and we leave room for blessing. And isn't that a wonderful thing?

* Divine inspiration.

March 29, 2020

We Are the World

Corona is a planet in our familiar solar system. And, like Earth, it really is a tiny dot in an immense universe. The nearest star to us is about 4.2 light years away. In contrast, to circumnavigate Planet Corona (Earth, too, for that matter) is a distance of a fraction of a light *second!* Tiny indeed. But to us even punier human beings, the planet seems an immense place, things being relative. Nevertheless, Planet Corona has become noticeably smaller in the last few weeks, and certainly more intimate, which emphasizes that it's shrinking.

The reason for this appears to be the fact that all of humanity is facing the same threats, hardships, and fears. Just as "My enemy's enemy is my friend," so a type of empathic identification is emerging from so many inhabitants of the planet being "in the same boat" (more on that later).

In the past, few of us have paid much attention to the concerns of people from a different country, or of a different race or religion. Perhaps we're not even doing it right now. But the fact is that we *are* sharing the same concerns, and if we reflect on our situation we might note that we are united with many millions and perhaps billions of others who share that situation.

In a very moving column in *Makor Rishon** this past Shabbat, Yair Agmon, who writes a weekly column in the newspaper, shared with readers that this March 20 was the fourth "anniversary" of the tragic birth of a stillborn child to his wife and to him. He had initially intended to devote the entire column to that subject but, in view of the current pandemic, he actually forgot his intention.

He did however share a very poignant and powerful thought. He wrote that four years earlier, after the heartbreaking event, he would walk in the streets and wonder how everyone could be doing their normal things and life could go on as usual when he was in so much pain and his own world had changed. This time around, he said, there was some comfort in knowing that his fears, his pain, and his challenges were shared with everyone. He ended by saying, "Without our realizing it, the plague has bequeathed us with empathy."

No. We are not yet in the place where lions are lying down with lambs. There is still more disunity and even hatred than makes God unhappy with us. And it is also true that it is only human nature to care most for your immediate family, followed by ever-widening ripples extending to the people of your city, country, religion, etc. But the ripples do, indeed, go on to encompass all of humanity and now we are experiencing that more powerfully.

For we are all made in the image of God. The *Tzelem Elokim,* the Image of God in which Adam was fashioned is the template for every inhabitant of Planet Corona. A beautiful commentary by the Maharal** in the *Chidushei Aggadot* on Parshat Vayera illustrates this point. When Hashem visits an ailing Abraham, setting the precedent for the commandment of Visiting the Sick, Abraham is distracted by the appearance of three "men" who are traveling past his tent. He runs to offer them food and drink, ostensibly leaving God's Divine presence in order to do so.

The question is asked, "How did he dare turn away from the Divine to deal with the mundane, from Hashem to three travelers whom he saw as three idolatrous Arabs." The Maharal answers that he did not actually turn *away* from Elokim, he merely shifted his gaze to the Tzelem Elokim within the "human" travelers, which shines within all the dwellers on Planet Corona.

I've had reason over the past few months to spend a lot of time in Shaare Zedek hospital with my sister and her son. A hospital is a great leveler of the playing field. Sicknesses, including coronaviruses, make no distinctions among genders, religions, ethnicities, and social status. In the hospital, all are represented as patients, as orderlies, as nurses and as doctors, and it is a model for tolerant coexistence and mutual support. Today, on some level, the whole planet is one big hospital and we all have some role within it.

Once, a very long time ago, all the inhabitants of the planet were "in the same boat." We refer to it as Noah's Ark. The predecessors of all humanity, of all peoples, all races, all nationalities, and all religions shared a space, experiences, and the common fate of surviving the Flood. Today, that Ark is Planet Corona.

* An Israeli newspaper associated with Religious Zionism and with the conservative right-wing.
** Rabbi Yehudah Loew (1525–1609), also known as the Maharal of Prague, was one of the outstanding Jewish minds of the sixteenth century.

March 31, 2020

Seeing and Vision

Not everyone on Planet Corona is actually a Coronian. There are many who are visitors and behave like tourists, and often clueless ones at that. What makes you a Coronian is a special way of looking at things and events, and the ability to focus on the present, as well as on the *little*, though in reality *big* things. It's also reflected in an ability to sense and actually "see" the "no things," those invisible but very real phenomena such as love, friendship, loyalty, curiosity, and above all, the Hand of God.

One of the items that makes it easier for non-Coronians to begin to understand and experience Planet Corona is a pair of eyeglasses that is issued to anyone who wishes when they arrive on the planet. It's a bit like the tinted spectacles that visitors who entered the Emerald City had to wear in the movie *The Wizard of Oz*. These spectacles have many interesting properties. They allow you to look within as well as without, to separate illusion from reality, and to focus, really focus.

And focus is so essential to life in general and to life on Planet Corona in particular. Because, unless you focus on something, or on someone, or on an experience, you don't really see, feel, or understand anything.

The Midrash says that *Adam Harishon*, the first Man, could see from one end of Creation to the other. It's not because he had such excellent eyesight, but because everything he saw was brand new since he viewed all of Creation with his own new eyes. And so he focused and didn't merely glance or overlook or ignore as we so often do when we've seen the same thing or person or had the same experience many times. He saw everything for the first time with adult eyes and understanding and therefore everything was special and awe-inspiring and so very beautiful.

I was told that in a biology class for non-science majors at Yeshiva University taught by Rabbi Moshe Tendler, the new students were asked to look into a microscope which was focused on a slide with a drop of water and describe what they saw. One said, "Well, I see these little funny-shaped things scurrying around." The question was put to them again, "But, what do you *see*?" The students tried again to describe the magnified water drop, but their answers didn't seem to hit the mark. And then Rav Tendler said, "Not one of you said that you see Hashem." *That* takes vision, understanding, and real focus.

How does that help you become a "real" Coronian? On Planet Corona, you need to look beyond the surface of things, to search for understanding of events even when they appear obvious. For example, one might say "It's obvious that technology is a really terrific thing after all. Where would we be today without our smart phones, Zoom, WhatsApp, Twitter, memes, etc., etc.?" But, looking deeper, there may be a message hidden beneath the surface. Perhaps with our Corona eyes or spectacles we discern something totally different.

Maybe we're being told in no uncertain terms: "You have become so attached to your hand-held technology. You have chosen virtual relationships over real relationships, myriads of Facebook 'friends' over a smaller but choicer number of true friends, time spent in front of screens over time spent with family. You've attended family get-togethers where all the guests were hunched over their devices and no one spoke to one another. You were even photographed that way.

"Others laughed at you and then did the exact same thing. So now you can have all the time you want with your devices but without real and present companionship. You locked yourself in your room to spend more time with your screens, now spend *all* your time that way. Perhaps you'll get out when you've learned your lesson."

Rebbe Nachman of Breslov said: "You are where your thoughts are. So put your thoughts where you wish to be." If we look within ourselves with our Coronian eyes or eyeglasses, we might note that we often dwell on dark thoughts and fears, imagining worst-case scenarios.

Studies have shown that people have a "negative bias," meaning that we tend to think negative thoughts twice as often as positive ones when we let our thoughts and imagination go where they will. But, if we recognize this and observe our inner processes, we can change that. We can focus on more positive outcomes and feelings, and thereby generate a greater sense of well-being.

Coronian eyes and eyeglasses also have filters. Just as masks can be of some use keeping in or out those nasty droplets containing coronavirus, we can learn to filter out destructive outside influences and messages that lead to negativity, discomfort, even fear. We can allow in only that which is wholesome, productive, and nourishing. The Kotsker Rebbe queried: "Where is Hashem? Wherever you let Him in." Our filters should always be open to the presence of God.

On Planet Corona, our enhanced vision should also help us visualize a better future. Not one that takes us back to where we were before we landed on this planet, to that which was familiar and oh too comfortable. But to a future where, with our new way of seeing, we can be in a place of reality, not illusion, with living and breathing friends and family instead of animated pixels on a screen and with a heightened consciousness of Hashem's presence in our lives.

Chapter Two

April 2020

April 1, 2020

Exit Strategy: Part 1

Being on Planet Corona is equivalent to working towards a PhD in Living Meaningfully. Many of us are absorbing such powerful lessons in empathy, family values, trust, stripping away of illusions, etc. However, Planet Corona is not a permanent residence and I doubt that there is anyone who would wish to remain here indefinitely.

However, we don't know how long we actually *will* be here. It appears that it will be some time yet. And while we are here, we should glean as much wisdom as we can concerning life, important values, the people with whom we share our home and planet and, most importantly, concerning ourselves.

But, IYH,* one day we will go home once again, so one of the things with which we need to occupy ourselves in order to make the best transition possible is to devise a good "Exit Strategy." Because, whenever it happens, we don't know what we will find when we do get home. Will it be like emerging from a shelter in London during WWII after a night's shelling to find that several homes on your block were hit by shells? Or will it be more like visiting Hiroshima the day after the bomb was dropped?

My totally intuitive guess is that it will be something in-between, but as usual the only honest response is "we just don't know." However, it's pretty certain that a *lot* will be different. What will it be like and how different will it be? Again, "we just don't know." Nevertheless, how we adjust and how we make the transition will depend a good deal on what we do now while still on Planet Corona.

For one thing, we will all need to be very resilient. We will almost certainly have to adjust ourselves to new realities. So, how do we work on our resiliency *now*? Well, we are faced with challenges here on a daily basis. How do we react to our families or within ourselves when things don't go either the way we expected or the way we wished? We face unprecedented challenges, and we can't merely wish them away. What happens to us is seemingly out of our hands. But how we react is very much within our power.

A friend of mine who was going through great difficulties some years ago said that she prays to Hashem to please make the road she travels smoother. I responded that I wished the same for her, but suggested that perhaps it would be more fruitful to *daven* (pray) for "better shock absorbers."

When we get home, we will still have the same family and friends, hopefully. How have we improved our relationships while here on Planet Corona? We've certainly had a lot of opportunities to hone our skills of patience, empathy, tolerance, kindness, and affection.

Even if we've only become better at rebounding from unpleasant situations to reestablish better communication and to repair bruised feelings, we are improving our chances of doing better when we get to the "other side." We need to be conscious of the fact that how we grow and improve now will have lasting consequences for our future off Planet Corona.

Have we worked on nurturing our trust in God? We have been made painfully aware that "We have no one on whom we can depend, other than on Hashem alone." Are we making any progress in moving from the depressing thought that we have no one and nothing on which to depend, to the reassuring one that Hashem is assuredly taking care of us? That all is in His hands. As we are. After this, we will need that assurance more than ever and that may well be our greatest source of security, support, and encouragement as we face our new realities.

And what of ourselves? Have we done inner work to try to understand why we are in this universal "time out?" Are we asking ourselves what we need to work on individually and within society so that the world that we rebuild after our sojourn on Planet Corona is a better one than the one we left behind?

In the cartoon *Calvin and Hobbes*, Calvin is a precocious but often obnoxious six-year-old who hates going to school. His defiant cry is "You can make me go to school, but you can't make me learn anything!" We've been sent to Planet Corona for a "time out" that has cost many billions of dollars while the cost in human life and pain is incalculable. Wouldn't it be a horrific and shameful waste of time, money, and humanity if we refuse to learn something while we are here?

If we take advantage of all the benefits to be gained from this very expensive education we are receiving at Corona University, perhaps we can emerge wiser, better, and more loving citizens of our old home when we return. May it be soon.

* God willing.

April 2, 2020

Too Much

And sometimes it's just too much. And with all the understanding and lessons that we are deriving from our sojourn on Planet Corona, and with all the coping mechanisms and humorous or informative videos and e-mails we're receiving... endlessly. And, with all of that, we're still on a strange and mystifying and often frightening planet. And it's unlike anything that even the most senior among us can recall. And we don't know when it will end. And we want to cry out, even before we get to the Seder, "Dayenu! Get me out of here!"

So, I was feeling that way this morning. And probably will again. I went to purchase a few items at my local *makolet** on Rechov Bilu in Katamon. Mostly, just to get out for a (very) short while. And I put on my mask and my gloves (I was really a sight!) and drove the few blocks and parked. The first thing that hit my eyes was a 6-foot-wide sign on a fence directly across from the store. It said "גם זה יעבור" (This, too, shall pass) in large and very colorful letters.

Underneath it were pictures of other items that have been and gone, such as a mastodon, an old-fashioned Victrola, a rotary telephone, and an old-fashioned bicycle, along with pictures of the virus (does anyone still not know what it's supposed to look like?!?) and a face mask. The sign did, in fact, lift my spirits somewhat. Someone clearly was trying to cheer me up. Personally. ("The world was created for me!") And they certainly had some success.

So, thank you, whoever you are. And thanks to all the people who are sending me those diverting, humorous, inspirational and often educational pictures, videos, poems, etc. Thanks to the people who are reading these letters and letting me know. And thanks to my husband who is making this as tolerable as it can be.

Thanks to friends and family who remain in touch and tell me "Take care of yourself" even if they remind me that I am in the more vulnerable segment of the population. Or to put it bluntly, I'm old! Thanks to the powers-that-be in Israel who, through their efforts, have helped our country be rated "The safest country in the world!" Thanks to health professionals in the country who are working tirelessly and with tremendous self-sacrifice to help us contend with this unprecedented crisis.

And thank You, Hashem. For so many years I've believed in You and Your love for us, and Your personal intervention in our history and on a daily basis. So, it's really too late in the day to change gears. Nor do I want to. So thank You, Hashem even though I don't understand. Not even a little. But I will try to grow from this experience and become a better person with improved relationships and priorities.

I don't know how long You have it in mind to keep us on Planet Corona and I certainly don't know what's waiting for us when we emerge, but while I am here I will continue to try to make the most of my time here. Sometimes to better myself. Sometimes, just to make it through. And to those reading this, I just wanted you to know that we are all in this together. With all the ups and downs and with all the fears and the joys.

Have a very wonderful Shabbat and Seder night.

* Corner store.

April 3, 2020

Exit Strategy Redux

The reason that we need to work on an Exit Strategy now while on Planet Corona is because we don't know the nature of what is awaiting us on "the other side." It may very well be chaotic and disorienting, and it could be that decisions will need to be made fairly quickly without a lot of time for careful deliberation. It's now, while we haven't a lot to do, that we can find some tranquility to pre-think and pre-plan. We may then be as well-prepared as it is possible to be in a unique situation.,

I've been told that Navy Seals—the elite members of the US Marines who are often assigned the most dangerous missions—undergo rigorous training before embarking on a mission. Naturally, that includes extremely strenuous physical exercises that take their endurance to the limit. But it also includes techniques of visualization whereby each Seal conjures up in his mind a "movie" of sorts in which he is performing in the mission with confidence and calm. By doing this repeatedly, he practices in his mind behaviors that he will absorb without actually having to *be in* the actual challenge and which he will be able to draw upon during the actual mission. But the essential element is that this preparatory work is done extensively *before* the actual crisis.

So, we on Planet Corona need to plan now, think now, evaluate now. One of the most important areas we need to work on is how we prioritize in all our "lives," those comprising our personal, familial, communal, national, and even universal frameworks. So many of our previous experiences no longer exist or do exist in a dramatically different way. We don't go to school or to work or, if we do, it's in an extremely altered way.

All of our human interactions, or nearly all, are taking place through our technological devices. We aren't going to shiurim, out for lunch, on a date, to shul, etc. Even, or especially, our interactions with those at home with us—spouses, family members, roommates—are different as we try to manage the 24/7 exposure to each other under very trying conditions, especially before Pesach!

We are worried, overworked or bored, emotionally overtaxed and, for the most part, trying to maintain some equanimity and essentially keep ourselves from killing each other (OK, just figuratively speaking… I think.) Are we learning anything from all this?

Several mornings ago, my husband was listening to the Israeli news on the radio. One of the hosts of the news program is Assaf. At one point, his voice seemed to fade for a little bit and then came back stronger. He explained that in the middle of the broadcast, which he was obviously doing from home, his young son needed his attention, so he went off to help him for a few moments. The other host said something like, "Really Assaf, you are *working* at the moment!" Of course he said it in Hebrew.

But I say *"Kol Hakavod*, Assaf," Good for you! Why shouldn't the needs of your child take precedence over the needs of your audience for once? Perhaps the priorities of work and family need a shift. When this is over, who knows who will have jobs, anyway. But, maybe it's time for workaholics to look at the faces of their children (they're probably doing a lot of that now, anyway) and consider rearranging their schedules in future for less work and more time with family.

Now that our schedules and our lives are being pared down to the bare essentials, can we look with greater honesty at the way we lived prior to landing on Planet Corona? We are probably the wealthiest generation ever, with more creature comforts, more luxuries, more material goods than ever before. We've turned those luxuries into necessities and have been pampered and spoiled beyond anything at any time in history.

Has all that made us contented or satisfied? Or just wanting more? Have we taken note of the extravagance and often the waste? We throw out enough food to feed many of the poorer nations of the globe. Is that what we want to return to? Or have we been given an opportunity to reconsider and re-evaluate?

Are our relationships what they ought to be? Do we gossip about others? Are we kind and generous? Do we even have time to foster true and deep friendships and relationships? And what of our relationship to God? Are our prayers mechanical? Are Shabbat and holidays much more about indulgence in food and clothing and less about the real spirit of the day?

If we think about it honestly, do we really believe that Hashem has been happy with our over-indulgences in the way we celebrate special occasions? And, most sadly perhaps, are we actually looking forward to going back to all that when this is over?

This year, our Pesach is going to look very different from those of the past. Much more like the original Seder night in Egypt with nuclear families gathered together in their homes unable to go out because of the plague of death outside their doors. Just the family members wondering about what they were about to face, where they were about to go. In the midst of a ritual that they barely understood because it was so new, so different.

They vaguely understood that they were free. But what did that mean and who was this leader they barely knew? And how to understand this Deity, whom they knew only through his

Power and Glory but not yet through His Love. The way that we on Planet Corona are seeing an almost unprecedented manifestation of God's awesome power, and yearn for His love and protection.

But we shouldn't model ourselves too closely on that first generation. Because we know that after they were freed from Egypt and wandering in the desert, they kept turning towards Egypt, tragically looking back with yearning to their years as slaves. Not really accepting that they were traveling to a far better place and would get there if only they didn't continue to desire a return to the past, to the familiar, as flawed as it had been.

We need to grow and learn from our experience on Planet Corona. This experience is our "crucible" where we are being purified by pain and suffering. We need *now* to rid ourselves of the dross of our previous lives, the hubris, the materialism, the misplaced priorities.

And then, IYH, we will emerge from *our* Egypt, not looking back longingly at "The Way Things Were," but—with optimism and renewed courage and faith in ourselves and our world—towards "The Way They Can Be."

Shabbat Hagadol Shalom!

April 6, 2020

Getting down to Essentials

There is something extra in the air on Planet Corona. No it's not the feeling of spring, although this is certainly the season for that. And it's not those nasty virus droplets, although regrettably there are too many of those. No, it's an additional element with an interesting property. We can call that element coronium and its quality is that it is "cor-rosive." Not in the usual way of causing physical corrosion. No, the air on Planet Corona is perfectly breathable (except for those noxious droplets).

But what the corrosive property does is strip people, objects, and events of illusion, pretension, masquerade, and hypocrisy. It then helps lay open the core reality of everything. Unfortunately, you may choose to blind yourself to the effect as it might force you to rethink or re-evaluate, and that might make you uncomfortable.

After all, everyone, including the emperor, really knew that he hadn't a stitch on. However, until forced to confront that fact by the little boy [in the story], it was easier and safer to pretend that the emperor was sumptuously clothed.

But isn't it better on the whole to live a real life rather than an illusionary one? It would seem clear that Hashem "thinks" so. Otherwise, why did he send us to Planet Corona with coronium in the air? We've been faced with the reality that we are, and have always been, *totally* vulnerable. To everything. With all of our progress in medicine, science, and technology we are not, in any essential way, less vulnerable than our ancestors.

Today, when I went out for a few minutes of last-minute shopping for Pesach, I looked again in wonder at the scene around me. Most people on the streets in masks and gloves; almost no cars on the road; no children playing outside; one person at a time allowed into the makolet. Who would have imagined such a scene just a few weeks ago?

But, in essence, that's the way it's always been. There's a lot in nature, in our air, that is inimical to health and normal life for humans. Only we are made in a miraculous way to be able to ignore that fact because of antibodies and all the added protections that our body is born with or produces. *"Rofeh kol basar u'mafli la'asot."** Now we know it.

We've learned to live within a routine, and it makes our lives more comfortable. Not only does the sun obligingly rise each morning but most other parts of our day also proceed almost as regularly. We make breakfast, go to work, the children go to school, we go to shul regularly (some more than others), we meet with friends and family. Routine. Which often leads to taking things for granted and a loss of gratitude and even wonder.

Only extraordinary events lift us out of our lethargy, things such as holidays, special occasions, vacations, travel to exotic places, etc. Or loss of those things and people we take for granted.

In a recent shiur, former chief rabbi of the British Commonwealth Jonathan Sacks suggested that the *Avot* and the *Imahot*** had to be barren so that the Jewish people would cherish family and children forevermore. We had to emerge from slavery so that we would always treasure freedom. Hashem is "forced" to deprive us so that we can learn to cherish and be grateful. But we could sidestep the deprivation if we could only learn gratitude for that which we take for granted and which is routine.

So now Covid-19 has stripped us of the trappings. We're without our all-important jobs, our friendly and familial contacts, without shiurim, without school, and without almost all the activities that filled the time slots of our daily routine. Which are also a significant part of our self-identity, how we present to others and even to ourselves. What's left? Just us. Just us in the world that God created and runs according to His plan, not our routine. Which gives us an unprecedented opportunity. We're down to the basics now. What will we re-adopt when this is over?

I was reminded of this idea today as I tried to finish cleaning my kitchen for Pesach. I have a smallish kitchen, but it's very practical. One feature is my counter space. I have a large amount for such a compact kitchen. Plus, I have a narrow spice shelf above my counter on one side which is almost 2 meters long. On it go spices, condiments, various coffees, and a few mugs and sundries.

Both my spice shelf and my counters accumulate a lot of stuff. So much so that even though my spice shelf is quite large, I still seem to run out of space. Before Pesach everything comes off my counters and spice shelf and they are left bare. After Pesach, it's time to put things back.

And that's the thing. Do I put everything back? Do I really need to crowd my spice rack with spices I thought I'd use more and have been sitting now for years and which I rarely if ever make use of? And the same goes for the clutter on my counters. After

Pesach, I could be much more selective as to what goes back. As I should be.

Of course, our lives are more complex than spice shelves and counters. But once we've cleared everything away, when we're down to our basic reality stripped of all accoutrements, what do we take back? We will need to go back to elements of our routine. But do we need all of it? Can we pare down the less important and increase the more important? In short, can we do it differently? Can we do it better?

On Planet Corona, there is a bell. It's known as the John Donne Bell. On it are inscribed words from his famous meditation:

> Any man's death diminishes me, because I am involved in mankind,
> And therefore never send to know for whom the bells tolls;
> It tolls for thee.

Donne's message was that all humankind is intertwined, and therefore any death means one less "*tzelem Elokim*" in the world and we must be touched by any loss. We are, in effect, made less by any loss of life. This idea derives from the traditional role of the church bell in proclaiming that someone had passed away.

But bells frequently had another role. They were sounded as an alarm to waken the populace to an impending danger. In that way, the bell is like the shofar that is sounded before the Yamim Noraim*** in the month of Elul to, in Rambam's words, waken the slumberer so that he is alerted to doing *teshuva* (repentance) while there is still time. Not to sleep through those crucial times. Until it's too late.

We, on Planet Corona must remember that the bell tolls for us with both meanings. We must be sensitive and caring for the pain and loss of life that has come with the present crisis. But we must also very personally hear the wake-up call so that this crisis can usher in a better time for the world and for each of us.

Note: As I was writing this, I was informed of the tragic loss of a good friend, Prof. Mark Steiner. Now, for me, corona has a face. The bell tolls for us all.

* Healer of all flesh and performer of wonders.
** The biblical Patriarchs (Abraham, Isaac, and Jacob) and Matriarchs (Sarah, Rebecca, Rachel, and Leah).
*** Days of Awe.

April 8, 2020

Love in the Time of Corona
(With Apologies to Nobelist Gabriel Garcia Marquez)

Spring, traditionally, is the season of Love. Popular songs proclaim it, Hollywood makes mega-bucks from it, and on Planet Corona spring and love are also intertwined. But it's not the spring of *April in Paris* (too dangerous to go there anyway), nor is it love as portrayed in popular entertainment. Rather, just like everything else here, it's love in its most basic, truest, and most honest form. It's the spring of Chag ha'Aviv aka Chag ha'Pesach* when Hashem rescued us from our bondage in Egypt and lovingly took us for His Chosen Nation. And by removing all the encrustations that have sullied the idea of "love," we find it here on Planet Corona revealed in its purest manifestations.

For so long the word love has been trivialized. We "love" that pair of shoes, that kind of ice cream, a particular type of exercise shoe, etc. At one time I worked in a shop that sold silver Judaica. Many of the items were beautiful and many certainly contributed to *hiddur mitzva*, beautifying a mitzva. People purchased goblets, honey dishes, and etrog boxes for special holidays, for bar mitzvahs, weddings, and other occasions. Sometimes, a customer would spend a long time comparing one Kiddush cup to another and I often heard, "Well, I do *like* that cup, but I don't *love* it." I had to resist the almost overwhelming urge to say, "Love your husband. Love your kids. You don't have to love a cup!"

And, certainly, the huge and widespread influence of popular culture has contributed significantly to the impression with which many of us grew up that love is sudden, breath-taking, overwhelmingly charged, and essentially self-centered. In magazine articles (usually for women, of course) that feature self-administered surveys to ascertain if you are really "in love," the questions all center around how *you* feel when you are with the object of your affection and what the (perhaps) beloved does for *you*. It's in our songs, "You Make *Me* Feel So Young," and certainly it's a mainstay of movies and theater.

The one exception that comes to mind is "Do You Love Me?" from *Fiddler on the Roof* where the theme is that years of working together, caring for each other's needs, and sharing experiences is "also" love. Yes "It's nice to know." And perhaps it's also significant that this popular song appeared in the context of life in a traditional Jewish shtetl. Though I would imagine that most modern theater and movie goers saw the song as rather quaint, sweet, and essentially old-fashioned and passé. Something for a past time, supplanted by the newer model.

However, on Planet Corona we can see the manifestations of real love if we but open our eyes and our hearts. No one here is going to "See a stranger across a crowded room" (*South Pacific*) but rather will be closed up with others for weeks on end. Here we experience the real love of our children and grandchildren when, instead of asking for our help in these difficult days, they forbid us from leaving our homes and insist on doing our shopping and errands.

We call people who've touched our lives in the past, but with whom we haven't spoken in years. Couples get married with barely a minyan** after having planned the once-in-a-lifetime extravaganza they had dreamed of. While others have postponed to wait until they can have the party. As a friend said, "I guess it depends on whether you are planning a marriage or a wedding."

I recognize that even on Planet Corona, it's not all lovey-dovey. The director general of the UN reported a significant world-wide increase in domestic violence. And, tragically, many have lost dear and beloved spouses and parents and are grieving. I paid two Zoom shiva calls yesterday and my heart is with the families. And there are those who will conduct a one-person Seder, probably for the first time in their lives.

Yael Unterman, an author and friend, wrote a beautiful blog about her voluntarily choosing to protect others and have a Seder on her own. She gave several suggestions as to how to weather the experience and one thing she emphasized was that there *will* be love at your Seder. The love of the people who are not present physically, but who are in your heart as you know that you are in theirs. The love of past generations who wouldn't be there in any case, but to whom you are still bound with ties of love.

Additionally, you are with yourself whom you hopefully love, thus fulfilling the dictum "And you shall love others as you love yourself," which is meaningless unless you do love yourself. And this is *not* self-centered, except in the most positive way. Egoistic love is self-indulgent, not self-affirming. And, adds Yael, never forget that the love of Hashem is there with you. "I am with [you] in adversity" (Psalms 91:15) It is precisely when you need Him the most that he comes to sit by your side with love and caring.

A misleading, but very popular and oft-quoted definition of love from a best-selling book then movie from several decades ago, suggested that "Love means never having to say you're sorry." Ridiculous, because it's quite the opposite. Love means that along with the words "I love you," the two most important sentences in a relationship are "Thank you" and I'm sorry." Said whenever appropriate—and they are often appropriate—they can help nurture and sustain any kind of relationship.

The word "like" has also become trivialized, especially lately, in its use within social media. But at least it is an active verb, even if the only action required is to hit a key! "Love" also has to be an active verb. It is what you do for and with the other that develops that relationship. Being "in love" is static and doesn't really take you anywhere. But "loving" in an active way, as it's developing here on Planet Corona, creates meaningful relationships and a deeper understanding of love.

Its activities have included neighbors helping neighbors, reaching out to others via whatever means are possible, davening for people you know and others who you don't know, but with a feeling of shared humanity. People are sharing their resources, making significant donations of money and goods to help others. And the list goes on. And all in the manner of *imitatio dei*, imitating Hashem's love for and goodness to His creations.

The gematria*** of *a-h-a-v-a* (love) is 13. Furthermore, the gematria of the name of God—*y-h-e-h*—which indicates His loving-kindness is 26, which suggests that holy love takes two people. If we focus solely on what is good for ourselves then we are only "half-humans." It's only when we realize "it is not good for man to be alone" (Genesis 2:18) that we rise to the level of what love really should reach towards.

On Pesach, we experience Hashem's overwhelming love for us. That is why we read Shir Hashirim (Song of Songs)—which metaphorically describes the loving relationship between God and His people—specifically on Pesach. Furthermore, Hashem "remembers" our loving actions at the time of the Exodus: "I recall the loving-kindness of your youth" (Jeremiah 2:2).

And if this year you miss feeling the love of those who are not with you, remember that Hashem's love can, and easily does, make up the deficit.

With love, from Planet Corona.

---

* The Festival of Spring, aka the Festival of Passover.
** Prayer quorum of 10 men.
*** An alphanumeric code in Hebrew of assigning a numerical value to a name, word, or phrase based on its letters.

April 10, 2020

The Family of Man

This particular letter from Planet Corona is one that I didn't really foresee writing and, in a way, I'm a bit ashamed that this is so.

I remember the first time that I heard the word Esperanto as it pertained to the idealistic international language. I was in grade school and it appeared in a line in a Purim play. We were told that Esperanto was an international language that almost no one speaks. Today, I Googled it and read up on its history. It was created in the late 1870s by a Polish-Jewish ophthalmologist from Bialystok. His purpose was to create a universal second language to foster world peace and international understanding. In his own words:

> The place where I was born and spent my childhood gave direction to all my future struggles. In Białystok, the inhabitants were divided into four distinct elements: Russians, Poles, Germans and Jews; each of these spoke their own language and looked on all the others as enemies. In such a town a sensitive nature feels more acutely than elsewhere the misery caused by language division and sees at every step that the diversity of languages is the first, or at least the most influential, basis for the separation of the human family into groups of enemies. I was brought up as an idealist; I was taught that all people were brothers, while outside in the street at every step I felt that there were no *people*, only Russians, Poles, Germans, Jews and so on. This was always a great torment to my infant mind, although many people may smile at such an 'anguish for the world' in a child. Since at that time I thought that 'grown-ups' were omnipotent, so I often said to myself that when I grew up I would certainly destroy this evil.

The present state of Esperanto is interesting, and you can look it up if you like and if you have the time (Ha!). However, I believe that there is an international language today on Planet Corona and it is common to billions of people. It is known as Coronese. It is a shared language of shock, pain, loss, and grief. It is a language of disillusion, of doubts, of worry and of fear. However, it can also be, and may already be, a language of brotherhood, caring, mutual responsibility, and a shared fate for the human race.

Historically, Jews have been understandably wary of their non-Jewish neighbors. It's an ancient, deeply entrenched attitude with much justification. Additionally, there has recently been a resurgence of anti-Semitism, exacerbated since the advent of the pandemic.

Many of us who are children of Holocaust survivors were raised with a measure of this antipathy. For while there were undoubtedly "righteous gentiles," they represented the exceptions much more than the rule. Consequently, many of us pre-judge non-Jews which makes identifying with them, even during a world-wide threat such as the coronavirus, difficult. This distrust of the "rest of the world" may be an understandable prejudice. But it is still a *prejudice*!

No doubt, there are historical dangers for Jews in letting down their guard amongst gentiles. However, there is also a tragic danger in distrusting all of humanity. Hashem is not our exclusive Deity, though we maintain that we have a special relationship accompanied by heavy responsibilities. All humans are Hashem's creations.

Two traditions from the Passover holiday point to this. At the Seder, when we remove a drop of wine from our cup as we recite the 10 plagues, we symbolically reduce our "pleasure" due to the pain experienced by our Egyptian task-masters from those very plagues.

Additionally, when we recite Hallel* during the last six days of Passover, we "reduce" it by leaving out several passages because on the seventh day the Egyptians drowned in the Red Sea. At that time, the Midrash tells us that Hashem forbade the angels' singing the joyous verses of Hallel, saying, "My children are drowning in the Sea, and you sing with joy?!"

We Jews, along with the rest of the world, are all part of The Family of Man and must never forget it. We cannot be Jews without being humans. Previously, I referred to the story of Abraham and the three travelers (angels) in Genesis 15. There, our hospitable forefather asks God to "stand by" while he waits on the traveling merchants because he saw the imprint of God's image on every human. A lesson for us all.

On May 6, 1937, Herbert Morrison, an American radio journalist, was broadcasting the launch of the Hindenburg zeppelin, when he witnessed the tragic explosion that cost the lives of many of the people inside. He was horrified and cried out, "Oh, the humanity…!" a phrase which has come down as the defining cry of the event.

Today, we on Planet Corona are all witnessing a devastation that dwarfs previous tragic events. This tiny virus is wreaking havoc on *all* the inhabitants of this globe. On our fellow humans of all races, religions, nationalities. We today are, indeed, speaking the same language.

To ironically misquote Shakespeare from the *Merchant of Venice*:

> Do not *all people* have eyes? Have they not hands, organs, dimensions, senses, affections, passions? Fed with the same food, hurt with the same weapons, *subject to the same diseases*, healed by the same means, warmed and cooled by the same winter and summer. If you prick us, do we not bleed? If you tickle us, do we not laugh? If you poison us, do we not die?

There will always be differences on our globe. They give color and variety to life on Planet Corona. And, unfortunately, it appears that there will always be conflict. But underneath it all we look forward to the day when we will all at least agree on one thing, that Hashem is the Father of all humankind. For the moment, let us feel the loss of all life. And join in hope for a better future.

So much loss. So many lives. So much prayer. Oh, the humanity!

* Chant of praise recited on some Jewish festivals.

April 14, 2020

Fed up

Today, I read a blog the title of which was "I'm *so done* with this pandemic! How about you?" And I wanted to answer, "Absolutely! Me, too!" Because, of course, sometimes I really am "so done!" I've been trying to make some sense of being on Planet Corona. Sometimes I succeed better than at other times.

You see, I'm an "outgoing" type of person. With both meanings. I have a pretty gregarious personality, *and* I like to *go out*! In fact, I warned my husband that if people of our "age group" are limited to leaving our homes only to purchase necessities, I'm going to start buying eggs *one at a time*!! (If, of course, you can find any!)

So what of the clarity of purpose and meaning that I've been experiencing on Planet Corona? Why, as recently as the first night of Pesach I felt the specialness of a Corona Seder with just the two of us sharing thoughts and ideas into the night. So, what's happened?!?

I guess, there's one thing about that aforementioned clarity that comes with residing on Planet Corona. It appears that just like clarity everywhere else and at all other times, it doesn't always seem *so clear.* Because clarity is in the eyes of the beholder and, as we have human eyes we will often see things as we wish to see them or as we are used to seeing them rather than as they really are.

Could there ever have been anything clearer to *Am Yisrael* than the immanence of God when He communicated to them directly on Mount Sinai? Yet, they worshipped the Golden Calf shortly thereafter. They fell back into their old ways of thinking and behaving. As we all do.

So, on Planet Corona (and we are still here, have no doubt) we can lose sight of what seemed to be so clear at the beginning. We can become impatient and even disgusted with what is, and must needs be, a long and often painful process. And we need to look with "corona eyes" at our situation and not with the eyes that for all our lives have revealed the world according to the ways we expect them to be.

We often create events, people, and things in our own image. In fact, we even create *gods* in our image rather than the other way around. We project our own proclivities, desires, attitudes, emotions, and therefore we see our own selves reflected everywhere rather than seeing things and people as they truly are.

One of the first recordings I heard after arriving on Planet Corona was by a rabbi who was addressing his own children. He likened this experience to the way one of his high school *rebbeim** disciplined his class. The rebbe would call on the guilty party and would be confronted with the typical whine, "What did I do?" The rebbe would send the miscreant to a room to think of what he had done and when he had clarified his misdoing to himself, he could come back to the class and sincerely apologize, after which he could rejoin his class.

The speaker explained that, in his understanding, Hashem was sending us to our room to give us time to reflect on how we have been misbehaving and, when we came to a proper understanding, we would be permitted to rejoin a "normal" life. He then went on to suggest several ways our society desperately needed to improve. And the thing is, I largely agreed with his analysis. His "misdeeds" were ones that I have thought of frequently in the past.

The thing is that, as time has gone on, *many* people have cited the "time-out" theory of what's happening here on Planet Corona. And everyone has his or her own pet theory. It's because of rampant materialism, unfettered globalism, too little "Imagine" (thanks for nothing, John Lennon), lack of faith, selfishness, the abuse of the environment (with Mother Nature calling a halt), hubris, and even the mistreatment of women (you knew that one had to show up somewhere!).

So everyone pulls out a favorite "soap box" subject and identifies Hashem's purpose with his or her own. And, who's right? Well, doesn't the question itself smack of *hubris*?! We can all be "right" (or wrong). There are countless areas that need improvement in our world. And, unless your idea of "improvement" is what the "other guy" can do better, they may all be worthy. That is, if it leads somehow to *self-improvement*.

On Shabbat of Chol Hamoed,** at our table, which has featured just the two of us for a while now, I challenged my husband by asking, "If you could focus on one area that we need to improve upon right now, what would it be?" After some thinking, he came up with the area that he would choose. But it appeared to be one of those objectives that he could have no influence on and was, in essence, what "they" should do.

So I further challenged him by saying that my question could only be answered properly if he found what he could do *himself* to further this goal. Evidently, he took me quite seriously and right after Shabbat actually implemented a rather powerful personal commitment to this project. I was quite impressed and gratified. Because he really absorbed the idea that if we propose an area that needs improvement, we also have to be the ones who take a step in that direction.

So, if you think that we are in a sort of universal "time-out" here on Planet Corona, and if you further believe that we have been sent to our rooms for reflection and for change, then let's please not waste this time. Commit to some area of self-improvement. It will all be to the good. And don't just leave it as a "resolution." Go further and create a plan for implementation. Then, implement what you *can* now and devise a plan for further application when the time is more favorable.

And then, hopefully, Hashem will allow us to emerge and will post a huge sign on the entrance: "Welcome Home. I've Missed You!"

* Rabbinically ordained teachers.
** The Intermediate Days of Passover.

April 17, 2020

Joy in the Time of Corona

I had planned to write a much longer letter today, but on Planet Corona, as well as elsewhere, *"Rabot machshevot be'lev ish, ve'etzet Hashem hi takum,"* "There are many designs in a man's heart; however, the counsel of God will prevail" (Proverbs 19:21).

My Erev Shabbat became very crowded with many varied and even contradictory pieces of news and emotions and events, so I am going to write a shorter letter today to friends and family (and, as always, to myself!) But I didn't want to go into Shabbat without at least letting you all know how much you all mean to me and how grateful I am to have you receive my "musings."

I wanted to share one thought which was encapsulated in a short inspirational address by Rabbi Eytan Feiner. He spoke before the last day(s) of Pesach and his message was a call to celebrate the *simcha*, the joy, of the chag as well as all chagim, and this year in particular. He further called on us to take the simcha of the chag into the period following this Pesach.

It's not that he implied that this would be easy. It's simply that it is desirable, necessary, and even obligatory. He said that sadness and depression are perhaps the most powerful weapons in the arsenal of the *yetzer hara*.* Out of depression and sadness comes loss of hope which often leads to destructive behavior and even sin.

The Netivot Shalom, in his essay on simcha, posits that to be *b'simcha* (joyful) is an obligation, and therefore we must strive mightily to achieve that state. He writes that if simcha were merely the reaction to positive life experiences or the result of an easygoing personality, it wouldn't be stressed as a state *to achieve*. It is a life-approach that must be attained by effort and a sense of well-being that will not be buffeted by every "ill wind" that blows.

It's also clear that being b'simcha is *not* an impossible-to-achieve requirement to be always smiling and cheerful. We are permitted, even sometimes commanded, to mourn at times and feel sadness.

But, despite events and circumstances that might lead to depression, we are obligated to be optimistic and to feel the security of Hashem's love and participation in all our life experiences.

So, whatever it takes to help you be b'simcha, read it, listen to it, participate in it, connect to it, talk about it, reach out for it, meditate on it, and absorb it.

A wonderful Shabbat to all of you and may you have a Shabbat of *menucha, v'simcha or la'Yehudim*, contentment, gladness, and light for all Jews (and everyone else on Planet Corona!).

* The evil inclination.
** From the Sabbath eve melodies.

April 20, 2020

Can't Visit? Re-visit!

On Planet Corona, there is no Ministry of Tourism (duh!). However, in its place we have the Ministry of Re-visiting. It's not physical re-visiting. No one actually goes very far except in their minds. And we don't just re-visit places (at least very nearby places), we also re-visit ideas, concepts, relationships, popular sayings and, perhaps most importantly, our inner selves. So, I would like to share with you some of my re-visiting of the last few weeks.

As mentioned above, we don't really go far in our physical re-visiting. Still, what we may miss in distance traveled we can partially make up in depth of experience. For instance, when I leave my home I usually go directly to my car parked behind the house. (By the way, we've never had a tank of gas last this long!!) So, I don't see the flowers, trees, and plants in the front of the house.

But, now that I go out on foot most of the time, I've noticed the lovely flowers, blooming and about to bloom, along our front walk. There is an orange tree that we planted several years ago, and we just noticed that it is full of orange blossoms that are budding and are quickly opening. I don't ever remember noticing them before. They're lovely.

I've also grown to appreciate more and more the apartment that we live in. Of course, I've always slept here, and hosted here. But much of the time I've been "on my way out!" But it's actually a very comfortable, spacious-for-two, practical place to spend all the time that we've been spending in it. I am very grateful to have this place to call home. I've probably never before been as cognizant of just how thankful I should be.

There are some notions that I have also re-visited. One was that Shabbat meals with just the two of us was something to be avoided as much as possible! Not because I ever doubted that I could spend very pleasant time with just my husband. We've often traveled on our own and I've always found him to be great company.

However, I love to host on Shabbat and chagim and have felt that the meal is somehow deficient without guests. But, surprisingly, I've found that the meals for "just the two of us" can be quite lovely with good conversation and we've even sung *zemirot*,* which due to our not great voices, we generally avoid.

And, if that was true about normal Shabbat and holiday meals, you can imagine how worried I was about the Seder! I had never in my life been at a two-person Seder. As soon as I was born I was at least part of a threesome! Surprise! It was lovely. I still look forward to larger Sedarim with children and grandchildren (especially grandchildren), but an intimate Seder is no longer to be dreaded.

I've previously mentioned that I have never seen myself as a writer. I speak and teach, but I've never written. Well, I find that I can and, in fact, I *do* write now. I've received some very nice feedback from others but, as I began this for my own need to express my ideas and feelings, I find that writing is a very useful and empowering outlet for me. Who knew?

Even my understanding of what makes me tick has been altered by the re-visiting I've done since I landed on Planet Corona. If someone had ever told me that I would be able to deal with an almost total house-bound existence with very limited interaction with others besides my husband, I would have laughed derisively saying, "You have to be kidding!"

This is not to say that I don't miss friends and family. I do. Greatly! Pixels do not make up for the real thing. But I am managing. And I think I'm managing pretty well. Most of the time, that is. I know others who have had similar experiences of surprising themselves about their capabilities.

And there are many sayings that I've revisited. But the one that I've thought about most recently is "There's no such thing as a free lunch." Of course, it still has its appropriate and useful applications. But one thing that I've come to appreciate on Planet Corona is that when so much of what we've become used to is reduced or gone, what still remains that is valuable and sustaining is also what's *free*!

We didn't pay to have life, health, or bodies that usually do what we ask of them. There was no charge for the *neshama*, the soul, that connects us to wisdom, spirituality, and to Hashem. The relationships that are supporting us during this crisis are not ones that can be measured in any cost-efficient way. If we have "invested" in them in any way, they have proved much more valuable than we could ever have imagined.

And the kindnesses that are all around us—those that are bestowed upon us by our fellow-man and those that God gifts us on a daily basis—are given with no anticipation of payment or repayment. With this in mind, I've also re-visited that old saw, "The best things in life are free." Even upon re-visiting, that one holds up very well!

* Shabbat melodies.

April 21, 2020

Yom Hashoah* on Planet Corona

I had already half-written the next Planet Corona letter (OK, it only existed in my head, but that's generally how these things get done). But, as today is Yom Hashoah I'm postponing that letter temporarily.

There is probably not a Jew on all of Planet Corona today who has not been affected in some way by the events in Europe of 1939–1945. After all, we weren't *born* on this planet. (Well, some of us were, but they are very tiny indeed!) There are many of us who are descended or closely related to people who survived and others who, tragically, didn't survive.

Being on Planet Corona does not erase our previous lives, rather it gives us perspective on those very lives. Our memories remain. And just as I hope and believe that Planet Corona can help us place our previous lives in a better perspective, it's also true that there are memories and shared history that can shed light on and give some perspective to our existence here on Planet Corona.

There are those who compare our situation with the experience of the Holocaust. They usually begin with some sort of disclaimer, but then proceed to compare. I understand that my personal experience of this crisis is probably less onerous than that of many others. I have a comfortable apartment, plenty of food, no full-time job, and no bored ADHD children.

I also am aware that one person's unpleasantness may be another person's nightmare. I don't care for spiders, but I don't have a phobia. That said, and not trying to negate the difficulties of our situation, I think we can only benefit by comparing our situation with the Holocaust, in realistic terms.

For one thing, most of us *do* have adequate food. A lot of my emails and WhatsApps wail about the woes of weight gain at this time. Just as there are the "Freshman 15" (the pounds that women at college traditionally gain their first year away from home), now it seems we have the Covid-19!

My own dear father, z"l, a Holocaust survivor from a shtetl in Galicia, spoke to us of being half-starved even before the war due to his family's poverty. He never even spoke about the dearth of food during WWII! But, we have all heard the stories of the battles over a piece of bread, the hoarding of food, the depths of starvation.

We have shelter. Generally, the kind of shelter that would have seemed luxurious to people living 100 years ago just about anywhere, without even having to refer to the Shoah. For that matter, we live in homes that are unimaginably superior to those of many people presently living on our planet. We've been dry, warm (or cool as the heat rises), furnished, with indoor plumbing, and running water. What luxury! Overcrowded, unheated, unsanitary barracks? Three-to-a-bed (if you could call it a bed)! Just imagine. You can't.

And we are adequately clothed. Abundantly clothed, if truth be told. Some of my friends are sharing with me the experience of "finally" having time to thin out their over-stuffed closets. Perhaps many of us (and our daughters) didn't get the new outfit (or outfits) for Pesach that we are used to, but I imagine that Anne Frank would have looked at our ample wardrobes as ones that only the wealthy could afford. And she was one of the more fortunate ones while in hiding. She, at least, had her own clothes. I needn't invoke the image of the kind of "clothing" worn by concentration camp inmates. Those images are etched deeply in all our minds.

We are also very likely going to survive this. Somehow. We have good reason for hope. Whereas Holocaust victims held on to the tiniest shreds of hope in order to be able to wake up in the morning.

And so that leads to the greatest contribution that the memory of the Shoah can make for us on Planet Corona. Previously, we've thought about what our memorials do for the martyrs and the survivors, and for the memory of that horrific time. But now those memories can do a great deal for *us*.

In his book *Happier*, Dr. Tal Ben-Shahar, whose class in Positive Psychology drew almost 2,000 students at Harvard (he has since come "home" to teach at IDC in Herzliya), says that one of the most important ingredients for a happier existence is the element of gratitude. He recommends keeping a gratitude journal in which you write down five things each day for which you are grateful.

I have started such a journal (again) during this crisis. In truth, those of us who pray daily already enumerate reasons for gratitude in the 15 *birchot hashachar* (morning blessings). But many of us, having recited these *brachot* so often, have become somewhat dulled to their impact. I recommend thinking anew of five things you are particularly grateful for on any given day and writing them down.

All of the benefits that were mentioned earlier in this letter—food, shelter, clothing, survival—only begin to cover the many things for which we should be grateful. Those of us who miss the chance to hug grandchildren should remember that we most likely will be able to do so again. We are not in the position of having to send children or grandchildren on a Kindertransport facing the likelihood that we might never see them again! Not to mention, how grateful we should be that we *have* grandchildren to hug. Not everyone is so fortunate.

We may be "enslaved" within our homes or at least within a few meters of our homes. I have no doubt that some rueful words on that were said at this year's Seder when we recited "*Avadim Hayinu,*" We were slaves. But we are certainly not enslaved in the way those who experienced the Shoah were!

One of the most moving books on the subject of the Shoah is *Responsa from the Shoah*** by Rabbi Ephraim Oshry. Rabbi Oshry lived in the horrific Kovno ghetto during the war and miraculously survived. He himself rendered halachic*** decisions during and after the war and had access to other responsa from that period. The fact that Jews even *sought* halachic guidance is a monumental testament to our Jewish and religious loyalty and steadfastness. It is well worth reading.

One very inspirational question came from an event during morning *tefilla* (prayer) in the ghetto:

One morning during prayer, Reb Avrohom Yosef, who was leading the congregation in the morning service, reached the blessing
"Who has not made me a slave," and shouted bitterly to the Mas-
ter of all masters, "How can I recite the blessing of a free man?
How can a hungry slave, repeatedly abused and demeaned, praise
his Creator by uttering 'Who has not made me a slave?'"

Others who participated in this service asked Rav Oshry for a
halachic decision. Should they continue to recite a blessing which
seemed a travesty, and should therefore be omitted, or is it forbidden to alter the service?

Rav Oshry responded:

One of the earliest commentators on the prayers points out that
this blessing was not formulated in order to praise G-d for our
physical liberty but rather for our spiritual liberty. I therefore ruled
that we might not skip or alter this blessing under any circumstances. On the contrary, despite our physical captivity, we were
more obligated than ever to recite the blessing to demonstrate to
our enemies that even if physically we were slaves, as a people we
remained spiritually free (p. 86).

Can we be any less grateful?
    May our memorializing of the victims of the Shoah be a blessing
for them, and, especially on Planet Corona, may the memory of
their experiences serve as an abundant blessing for us all.

* Holocaust Remembrance Day.
** New York: The Judaica Press, 2001.
*** Matters of Jewish law

April 23, 2020

Time Out

Those of you who might remember previous "Letters" (Don't feel bad. I can't always remember what I wrote either!) may recall that I once referred to a talk by a rabbi wherein he drew an analogy to our present experience. He compared our situation in the present crisis to that of a misbehaving student sent by a rebbe to another room to clarify to himself what he had done wrong. Only then would the wrong-doer be permitted to rejoin the class after sincerely apologizing for the wrongdoing. A version, therefore, of "time out."

So, in this analogy, we are in some sort of universal "Go to your room and think about what you've done." In fact, I believe that there is truth to this. The Gemara (the Talmud) states that if someone reaches into a pocket for a certain coin and ends up taking out a different one, that relatively minor inconvenience should cause the person to review his actions to see if he has sinned in some way.

Well, what the world is experiencing now is infinitely greater than the aforementioned "inconvenience!" Mustn't we then use this opportunity to review our actions, ideas, perhaps misplaced priorities? I would like to take the analogy one step further.

What if the student is sent to the other room 15 minutes before the end of the school day? Chances are he might choose to just wait it out. He could be pretty certain that he'd be allowed to go home with a very good chance that he could just "go back to normal" the next day.

But what if the student actually feels bad about having displeased the teacher? What if he actually would like to review his actions and discover what his failing was? (OK, OK, I know that this is really far-fetched in the real world. But this is my letter and I can direct it as I choose!) That student might not *want* to leave the room to which he's been sent! It's possible that he might really desire to fix what he messed up and "clean up his act."

A very popular Torah teacher once told me that she partly owes her interest in Torah teaching to a teacher she had in junior high school. It seems that she was a less-than-perfectly-behaved student and was therefore in the position of being asked to leave the class multiple times. However, this rabbi, her teacher, did not just send her out of the room. He gave her research on some Torah topic to complete before she could come back. And she found that she enjoyed it very much! She credits these "punishments" (and the teacher who imposed them) with her life-long love of Torah learning and teaching.

The problem is that even people who believe that changes need to be made don't usually agree on what changes these happen to be. We all seem to have different "soap boxes." But, you see, that's OK. There are probably *many* things that need fixing—globally, nationally, and personally. But the thing is, you need to think of something that *you* need to fix.

It doesn't have to be huge or seem to have global significance. Small actions, like small viruses, can have monumental consequences. And the time to think of what needs fixing is *now* before we leave Planet Corona where we've been given an opportunity for this introspection.

The idea that seemingly small actions can have huge consequence is a subtle theme of Megillat Ruth which we will read in a few weeks. The story in the *megilla** appears to be a simple one that affects only a few characters in one city. The actions are modest, understated, and discreet. But the last word of the megilla is the name "David" signifying the beginning of the true monarchy of Israel which will culminate in the coming of Mashiach** ben David, may it be soon. Quite a momentous outcome stemming from what appear to be far from earth-shattering events!

We can't know what the consequences may be of our actions and our changes. Nevertheless, we are not accordingly exempted from trying to work on ourselves. But more than that, we need to work on a plan of action to actualize our resolutions in order to ensure that they don't remain "just" resolutions.

This is so vital because it is so easy, too easy in fact, to just "go back to normal," to revert to our previous ways of doing things and wasting this opportunity to make ourselves and our world a better place. In fact, for many residents on Planet Corona this is what they actually look forward to. But even for those who hope for change, the danger of reverting is very great indeed.

Rabbi Yisroel Besser, who writes a column called "The Real World" in *Mishpacha Magazine*, tells of the Machnovka Rebbe, a tzaddik (righteous man), who many years earlier had been sent to Siberia. He had suffered years of cold, hunger, loneliness, and privation. When his wife was finally able to come to him, she brought clothing, a warm blanket, and some food. Yet, when the Rebbe saw her he screamed out, "I am starving for a Yiddishe vort [Jewish word]! Please say a *bracha* [blessing]—I haven't said 'Amen' in such a long time!"

When they were able to move to Bnei Brak, where he is privileged to have many minyanim and opportunities for communal learning and prayer, he and his wife maintained a custom where she would come to him every morning to recite the *Birchot Hashachar* and he would answer "Amen." They did this so that he would never forget the hunger and pain he felt at a time when he could not do so.

Rabbi Besser then goes on to confess that in Montreal, where he lives, permission had just been given for minyanim to take place outside as long as people remained on their own porches. For the first time in over a month, Rabbi Besser was able to daven with a minyan! What joy! Imagine his chagrin when he found himself reaching for his cell phone by the time they reached *Aleinu*.

How quickly the fire of inspiration can be dulled, if not quenched. Without a plan of action on how to implement our good intentions, we may find we have wasted our time on Planet Corona. What a shame.

Each of us need not look to change the world. In any case, we have no control over the outcome of our actions. However, inaction is not an option. Let's not fritter away our sojourn in "time-out." We neither can nor wish to stay there forever. Not even on Planet Corona.

* Scroll.
** The Messiah.

April 26, 2020

We Don't Know

I hesitate, for the first time, to use the full name of Planet Corona. Frankly, I don't know about you, but I am getting rather tired of the "C" word. After all, on Planet Earth, we hardly spoke of it at all unless we were involved somehow in one of the earth sciences. There are undoubtedly environmentalists out there who are thinking, "That's just the problem! We haven't been speaking enough about Planet Earth. Now look what's happened!"

Nonetheless, it's all that we hear about on the news, see on videos, read in the papers, and receive on social media. It's the subject of nearly every phone conversation and even of many of the inspirational shiurim (classes) coming to us on Zoom. Torah lessons on the weekly portion all attempt to connect with Covid-19 in some way. Last week with Tazria/Metzora,* it wasn't very difficult.

But whether we care for the name of the planet or not, we are still here. Others have shared with me that somehow this past Shabbat was unusually difficult for some reason. Perhaps because we were so occupied prior to Pesach with preparations and because our children were home for some time before the chag we put off a recognition that this was to be more of a long haul than we initially thought.

Well, as we used to say, "*Nafal ha'asimon*," the penny dropped! I guess, like many "prophecies" which are only understood in retrospect, this one meant that we *would still have corona even after Pesach*!

But perhaps that's just the point. Perhaps there's so much to say because Planet Corona is much more complex than anyone imagined. I have found these days that the most common three-word phrase employed by anyone, big or small, world leaders and regular citizens, even by those in the worlds of science and medicine is, "We don't know." And, unfortunately, if anyone takes the plunge and says something suggesting that they *do*, it rapidly becomes clear that, really, they don't!

It's a humbling experience for those willing to be humbled and even for those less willing. But if Planet Corona is not easily understood, that shouldn't surprise us. We ought to be used to it. After all, Planet Earth is far more complex, but also more fascinating, than most of us have taken the time to notice. When we say that Hashem's "works are great," most of us don't begin to understand a tiny fraction of what that means.

There's another similarity between the two planets that needs to be understood. It is that, just as different earthlings living in different areas of the globe in differing socio-economic realities with very different access to education experience life on Earth in radically different ways, so it is on Planet Corona. Everyone's experience of this new existence is unique.

I have had reactions to things that I've written that have emphasized that my reality is often far different from someone else's. I am reminded of a poem that I read many years ago called "The Blind Men and the Elephant" by John Godfrey Saxe. I think it's worth reading. At least, as worthy as much of what we actually are reading these days!

It was six men of Indostan to learning much inclined,
who went to see the Elephant (though all of them were blind),
that each by observation, might satisfy his mind.

The First approached the Elephant, and, happening to fall
against his broad and sturdy side, at once began to bawl:
"God bless me! but the Elephant is very like a wall!"

The Second, feeling of the tusk, cried: "Ho! what have we here, so very round and smooth and sharp? To me 'tis mighty clear, this wonder of an Elephant, is very like a spear!"

The Third approached the animal, and, happening to take the squirming trunk within his hands, thus boldly up and spake: "I see," quoth he, "The Elephant is very like a snake!"

The Fourth reached out his eager hand, and felt about the knee. "What most this wondrous beast is like is mighty plain," quoth he, "'Tis clear enough the Elephant is very like a tree!"

The Fifth, who chanced to touch the ear, said; 'E'en the blindest man can tell what this resembles most; deny the fact who can this marvel of an Elephant is very like a fan!'

The Sixth no sooner had begun about the beast to grope, than, seizing on the swinging tail that fell within his scope, "I see," quoth he, 'the Elephant is very like a rope!"

And so these men of Indostan disputed loud and long, each in his own opinion, exceeding stiff and strong, though each was partly in the right, and all were in the wrong!

So oft in theologic wars, the disputants, I ween, rail on in utter ignorance of what each other mean, and prate about an Elephant not one of them has seen!

So it is on Planet Elephant. No, no, I mean Planet Corona. Our experience of it will depend on many things. But unlike the blind men of Indostan we must not dispute "loud and long" another's experience and reactions. On Planet Corona, as well as on Planet Earth, we need to be more sensitive to differences and recognize that people view similar experiences in very dissimilar ways.

We have found out that all of us have much in common. For one thing, we are all susceptible to this virus and are finding the restrictions of our new life difficult. However, what exactly we find difficult and to what degree and what lessons, if any, we are taking away from this monumental experience depends on many variables.

Hashem miraculously made every single person who has ever lived different from every other. That is as much a miracle on Planet Corona as on Planet Earth. We must never forget that.

* The weekly Torah portion that deals with disease.

April 27, 2020

Yom Hazikaron on Planet Corona

On Planet Corona, it is also Yom Hazikaron, the Day of Remembrance. I have been watching the televised commemoration arranged through OneFamily, the organization that helps the families of victims of terror. I found that the program was led by Orit Mark Ettinger, the daughter of Rabbi Miki Mark, Hy"d,* who was killed in a terror attack which also left his wife Chavi and several children wounded. Rabbi Mark was the son-in-law of a very dear friend and mentor of mine, Ayelet Batt, and suddenly this whole event became more personal.

The program featured parents, siblings, and children of terror victims sharing memories and feelings of loss with the rest of us who may be fortunate enough not to have experienced this painful experience up close. The loss of a beloved family member or friend is heartbreaking.

During this present crisis, we have come face-to-face with this phenomenon more and more. Only the enemy now is not a human terrorist or an enemy soldier. It is a virus that doesn't choose its victims by any criteria other than proximity and susceptibility. But it also leaves destruction and grief in its wake.

This is by way of telling those of you out there who are receiving my "Letters" how much I appreciate all of you. Any kind of loss or pain is helped when you sense that somewhere "out there" are people who care. OneFamily lovingly embraces the grieving families and lets them know that they are not alone. On some level, albeit a very different level, any pain, any concern can be eased by having others share in it in some way.

These are, indeed, very difficult times. I do not in any way want to compare the hardships that most of us face today with those of the families of terror victims or fallen soldiers. However, the basic human need for empathy, caring, and a listening ear is universal in many diverse situations. And it is a service that we may render to each other, enriching and comforting one another.

When I began writing my "Letters," I did it mostly to help myself make some sense of the events of the past few weeks. Yet, I didn't keep it as a diary under lock and key. I chose to share it with others because it has been comforting to me to know that I have such wonderful family and friends "out there" on Planet Corona with whom I feel I *can* share these thoughts, ideas, and feelings.

I wanted each one of you who receives this to know that I value, more than I can say, your presence in my life. I know that at the receiving end of each of my "letters" is a person whose opinion I value and whose friendship I cherish.

There is a lot of "loss" these days. Loss of routine, income, security, health, and, most tragically, of lives. But, even within this painful reality there needs to be gratitude and appreciation for community, family, and our wonderful Jewish people. And much gratitude to Hashem Who has provided all of this to comfort us at this time. And, of course, Hashem is the great Comforter who has never abandoned us in times of trouble and never will!

May the memory of all those lost to war and terror be a blessing for their families and for all of the People of Israel. And may we all continue to be there for one another even if, at present, it is difficult to do so in person. Every one of us is loved by Hashem. Therefore, just as our Parent loves us, we must love each other.

And care for each other. And listen to each other. We are all in this together.

* May Hashem avenge his blood.

April 28, 2020

Humanogen

On Planet Corona, there is an element in the air we breathe (in addition to oxygen, hydrogen, nitrogen, etc.), which is known as H^0 (aka "humanogen"). Let me explain its main property. It fills all residents of the planet with one of two dissimilar qualities which stem from the same source. The source is the sense of our own human-ness, our limitations, our dependence, our vulnerability.

The two qualities that can stem from it are humility and low self-esteem. We can adopt the quality of humility and be in the same league as Moshe Rabbeinu, "the most humble of men," or we can be dragged down by low self-esteem and join the ranks of a Cain who, feeling that he wasn't worthy of Hashem's love, turns to violence and kills the brother whom he sees as the cause of his low feelings and position.

We are certainly inhaling large quantities of H^0 here on Planet Corona. We receive daily lessons in our vulnerability, our dependence, and our limitations (including the many that are imposed upon us for our own good). We are learning that we are not as much in control as we thought, not as knowledgeable as we had believed, not as "safe" as we had worked so hard to become. We have all discovered that what we *don't* know far outstrips what we do.

And that should fill us with good, healthy humility. Humility to realize that no one has all the answers. Humility to understand that no one person has more intrinsic value than any other. The virus couldn't care less. Humility to recognize that, indeed, *Ein od*

Milvado. That humility could help bring us together, with greater empathy for our neighbor, no matter where that neighbor resides.

Or these inhalations of H^0 can lead to depression, lowness of spirit, a feeling of helplessness. Those feelings, often stemming from low self-esteem, can lead to destructive behaviors, among them violence. Unfortunately, people who don't think much of themselves frequently believe that the fault is with others and that can lead to behaviors such as *lashon hara* (malicious gossip), bullying, and even to verbal or physical abuse. And, sometimes, the resulting violence can turn inwards with terrible results.

Both possibilities, and they both exist here on Planet Corona, derive from the element H^0 which we breathe in. Perhaps I should explain the symbol for the element. Of course, the "H" is for "humanogen." But the superscript, "0" (zero) is connected to mathematics. For the non-mathematicians, a superscript is that small number above a number or mathematical symbol that indicates the "power" of that number or symbol. Therefore, 2^2 means 2 to the second power, or 2 squared $= 4$, and 2^3 means 2 to the third power, or 2 cubed $= 8$. And so on.

However, any number to the zero power $= 1$ no matter how large the number is, so that 2^0 and $34,647^0$ both $= 1$! Which, on Planet Corona, means that no matter how big an "H" you are, no matter how old, how smart, how powerful, how wealthy, you are still "only" *one* member of the human race. No more. But also, no less.

This is something that we all know within our *neshama*, our soul, but it doesn't always reach our consciousness or our actions. If we truly understood this, we would also understand that we are all singular, not only in number but also in our essential selves. Every Coronese has unique ideas, relationships, ways of communicating, and approaches to life. That's not to say that all ideas are equally useful or even ethical, but certainly more than *one* approach can be valid.

"My way or the byway" may rhyme, but it is also very destructive of family relationships, communities, and even nations. This is a lesson that I personally am coming to grips with. And my stay on Planet Corona has helped me to begin to come to terms with this understanding.

Tonight is Yom Ha'atzmaut, Israel's Independence Day. Jews around the world will be celebrating, or not celebrating, this day for many different reasons. And more than one reason has some validity and is based on something.

For some, that "something" might indeed be a lack of knowledge or understanding. However, it may also derive from a *different* and an alternate way of reading halacha and/or history. I do not have to agree with your outlook or your approach. I am not obligated to do so. However, I am obligated to love and respect you as my fellow.

Tonight, I heard a beautiful idea from Dr. Avivah Zornberg concerning the idea of *Ve'ahavta le'rayacha kamocha*, Love thy neighbor as thyself. She pointed out the difficulty in this command and quoted the Ramban (Maimonides) who says that it is an exaggeration, and he therefore limits the scope of the requirement. But, she continued, we must remember that Hillel said that these three words are the entire Torah and the rest is commentary.

She suggested that, while it is certainly true that *Ve'ahavta le'rayacha kamocha* is a demanding requirement, especially if understood in its fullest sense, i.e., loving the other to the extent that you love yourself, it is still the underpinning of everything else. We must always keep in mind that ideal even if it is difficult to achieve. It is said that Hashem dwells in the space between one Jew and another. And He's not nearer to one or the other.

I do not know where we will be when this is (finally) over. There are those of us who have believed that "the world" needs to make some huge changes from our pre-corona lives in order to restart our world properly. I once thought so too. That seems a long time ago.

Today, after some deep breaths of H^0 I have to say that I don't know if there will be some cataclysmic change, some universal movement towards something better. Maybe there will be. Maybe not. But much can also be accomplished by many individuals making changes in themselves. Maybe that won't shake the world. But maybe it will.

> When I first started learning *mussar*, I became angry at the whole world, but not at myself.
> Afterward, I became angry at myself also.
> Finally, I became angry only at myself, and I judged the world *l'chav zchus* (to the side of merit)

> ~ R' Yisroel Salanter, ztz"l.

Chapter Three

May 2020

May 3, 2020

Pandemic as Rehab Intervention

In one of my earlier, pre-Pesach "letters," I compared the exit strategy from Planet Corona at the end of our present crisis to the way I deal with my spice shelf. Of course, I had no idea that this much later we would still be as deeply within the crisis as we are.

The spice shelf story had to do with the fact that I have a very wide, deep, and overcrowded spice shelf, all of which I clear away before Pesach. I went on to say that this year, post-Pesach, I intended to review my spices and condiments when I unpacked them and then decide which ones I would put back on the shelf, which could be put elsewhere for occasional use, and which should be discarded.

The comparison to our crisis was that, like my spices, we have put so much of our personal, national, and even universal lives "in storage" for this period. We might then wish to contemplate, both now and upon exiting, which pre-corona ideas, activities, and acquisitions we wish to go back to "as is," which we need to trim or modify, and which others we can do without entirely or replace with better options.

A few days ago, someone sent me a quote from a lengthy essay by Charles Eisenstein, an author and public speaker, who is also an original thinker. His introduction caught my attention:

Covid-19 is like a rehab intervention that breaks the addictive hold of normality. To interrupt a habit is to make it visible; it is to turn it from a compulsion to a choice. When the crisis subsides, we might have occasion to ask whether we want to return to normal, or whether there might be something we've seen during this break in the routines that we want to bring into the future. We might ask, after so many have lost their jobs, whether all of them are the jobs the world most needs, and whether our labor and creativity would be better applied elsewhere. We might ask, having done without it for a while, whether we really need so much air travel, Disneyworld vacations, or trade shows.

While I don't agree with all the areas of improvement that Eisenstein chose to focus on in his essay, his suggestion that this is a time to question what has been "normal" and deliberate alone and with others whether a "new normal" is called for resonated with me.

We do appear to be at a crossroads of sorts where we have an opportunity to re-evaluate our world, globally, nationally, and personally and see what we should keep, what we can adapt, and what we could discard.

However, we need to be cognizant of the potential dangers that can arise from post-crisis attempts to correct previous wrongs. The Communist Revolution was born in reaction to a society with immense disparities in wealth and power. There was much to inflame the revolutionary fervor. But today we are aware of the horrors of the communist era, particularly the murder of millions of Soviet citizens under Stalin's dictatorship. The cure was nearly as horrifying as the disease. And, in fact, as described in the dystopian novel *Animal Farm*, the cure often adopted the trappings of the original disease.

It may be very tempting, following the cataclysmic awakening that many in the world are experiencing, to wish to essentially re-create world society and to form or join highly ambitious movements to bring about world-shaking changes. And there may indeed be a place for far-reaching and deep change.

However, we need to be careful not to be attracted by demagoguery that may come in the guise of idealism. We mustn't forget that individual efforts, if they are multiplied by many individuals, can also generate important results.

Too often I read and hear that there are those who seem to believe that just getting rid of one politician or another will usher in a glorious new era. This approach may not be as destructive as the possibility of the rise of a demagogue, but it is, at the very least, naïve. No one person is either the full answer to how to emerge from this crisis or the sole obstacle to doing so.

It will take much more individual effort than simply voting "the right way" to make any real changes. It's not only lazy and probably useless, but may even be dangerous as we place or misplace our trust in any humanly flawed individual, with or without a "hidden agenda."

How we emerge (may it be soon!) will probably depend a lot on how much change we, individually, are willing to make in our own lives. Rather than say that the whole world must take care of the poor, the weak, and the underprivileged (a very worthy undertaking) we each should give more charity, set aside time each week to do acts of *chesed* (lovingkindness), make phone calls to those who are home-bound, etc.

If you think that the world is far too involved in materialistic pursuits, coupled with the need for instant gratification, don't wait for governments or leaders to make the needed changes. I sincerely doubt that this can be legislated. Look at your own probably ample "stuff" and ask, "Do I really need to buy a new pair of shoes, another gym outfit, the new hot lip color, the latest iPhone?" As you know, the list is endless!

The Gemara warns us that the person who is focused on material acquisitions will never attain half of what he or she wants, no matter how wealthy they become.

Do we need to fix the environment? Check out your own carbon footprint. Bring on world peace? Who are *you* not speaking to? Reduce racial hatred? Check out your own biases. (Of course, yours would be legitimate biases, right?!) You get the idea. It's true that you mustn't miss the forest for the trees. The big picture is important to keep before you. But without trees, i.e., individuals doing their utmost, there wouldn't be any forest.

PS: If you are curious as to what I did with my spices after Pesach, the fact is that I looked at each one as I returned them to the shelf, discarded very few, and arranged the remaining ones (the majority) in a more user-friendly way. It's true that I didn't in fact reduce the number of my spices and condiments much but, as I already owned these items, I decided that this was a free splurge and, after all, variety is the spice of life!

May 4, 2020

It's Not Easy—an Understatement

When we first arrived on Planet Corona (seems like years and years ago!), I imagine that there were those of us who experienced a frisson of excitement. (Mea culpa!) It was clear, almost from the beginning, that we were now living in an extraordinary period of history.

Something earth-shattering was happening and we were all part of it. This would be talked about, written up, and analyzed for a long time to come. And *we were there*! "Yes, sweetie, Savta was only a teenager during the Great Corona Crisis, but I remember it like it was yesterday!"

But, no doubt, at the back of our minds was the caveat, "Well, this might be a nice place to visit, but I wouldn't want to *live* here!" However, it looks as if we are likely to live here for some time to come. The length of our "visit" is not at all in our hands. In fact, no one knows just how long our sojourn (incarceration?) will be. And, for many of us, this has been and continues to be an increasingly difficult period.

I have to admit that, although I am not by nature a particularly stay-at-home type of person, my own experience has been rather benign. My husband and I have a comfortable apartment, plenty of food, no job to get to, and no bored, difficult children to contend with. However, I am increasingly aware that my experience is far from universal. Probably, just the opposite.

In the last edition of *Makor Rishon*, the Hebrew-language newspaper that comes out every Friday, there was a short opinion piece by a young woman venting her understandable frustration. Loosely translated and paraphrased, she said the following:

> If you are in isolation with your family or in solitude, you probably haven't been able to escape the new " flower children" of all types who are trying to persuade us that there is some rationale to this horror. It goes from "Hashem is trying to give us *mussar* [an ethical lesson]" to "This is a gift, teaching us to appreciate simplicity, togetherness, quiet…" One imagines that these ideas are coming from single people with financial security whose biggest concern is that the take-out food delivery is late.

At this point you could actually hear her voice go up many decibels to: "*Chevra* (friends), enough!! *No one* is trying to give us any messages! And there is *nothing* positive about this plague!…" She then continues on in this vein. And, as I may be one of the "flower children" she is alluding to (though she would not have been likely to read my Letters), I feel I should respond with sympathy and understanding. Because her experience is not mine and she is likely faced with enormous challenges that I do not have to contend with.

So to her and many others, I wish to say: "You truly have my sympathy. My way of dealing with this situation, through trying to make some sense of things and writing about them, is the manner in which I can best deal with this crisis. I totally understand that it's not your way and I sincerely feel for what you are going through. So this letter, Noa Angel (the columnist's name), is for you and for others who are facing difficulties, challenges, and tragedies at this time.

For my dear sister, who has spent more time *in* the hospital than *out* of it with her special needs son. Though he does not have corona (it's actually something more serious), her situation has been exacerbated by the present situation, including, but not limited to, the fact that I can no longer visit her there every day to keep her company.

For a friend whose beloved husband was taken from his family and friends due to Covid several weeks ago. He was a very special person, professionally and personally, and he is and will be missed terribly. But, as our Sages remind us, the loss is felt most painfully by the remaining spouse.

For my sweet daughter-in-law who made aliya about seven months ago and whose mother has been taken ill across the ocean. Although she is aware that even if she were still in the US, she would not be able to be with her mother in the hospital or rehabilitation facility, she still feels the distance and the pain knowing that her mother is facing all of this alone.

For my *mechutenet* [in-law] who lives in Israel, whose 90-year-old mother also succumbed to Covid-19 in New Jersey, also alone, and who "sat" a Zoom shiva in her home and was "visited" by on-screen consolers.

For the friend who had Covid-19 and spent over three weeks in a corona facility alone most of the time, including Shabbat and Seder night. Though she felt fine for much of the time, she couldn't manage to get two negative tests in a row allowing her to emerge from isolation. (I guess sometimes two negatives do, indeed, make a positive!)

For the family of Judge Noach Dear of Brooklyn, who recently succumbed to Covid-19 at the age of 67. He was a friend of our family when he was just setting out on his career.

For the family of Rabbi Yeshayahu Heber, founder of Matnat Chaim, an organization that encourages the voluntary donation of a kidney. Several days ago, he succumbed to Covid-19, leaving behind his extraordinary work in saving many hundreds of lives through facilitating kidney donations in Israel. My own nephew just recently donated a kidney, and the family is very proud of him.

There are so many others, some I know of and many, many more that I do not. I can't possibly know the huge challenges that many are facing on a daily basis. Challenges that are exacerbated by the fact that no one really has any idea when and how this will end. Or if "end' is, in fact, a word with too much finality. As if there really could be some crisp and distinct border between pre-corona and post-corona.

I have a compelling need to derive some meaning from all of this. Even as I am aware that I cannot possibly ever know what the deepest reasons are. Still, I attempt to imagine possible directions for my thoughts and feelings. And I continue to share these thoughts and ideas with others. Perhaps they will find some comfort or meaning in some of what I write. Perhaps not.

But for all of those for whom this has been and continues to be a stressful, challenging, and even tragic time, I send you the only words I can think of to say at this time, "I am so very, very sorry."

May you all stay healthy and sane and may we all emerge from this with, at the very least, a greater sense of understanding of and sympathy for our fellow residents of Planet Corona.

May 5, 2020

Upside-down World

Perhaps the most extraordinary elements on Planet Corona are the unusual and unexpected views. They can manifest as shifts in one's visual apprehension of people and objects. For instance, I don't believe that I have ever paid as much attention to the beautiful rose bushes just a few meters away from the bottom of my staircase. They are quite stunning when you really stop to look at them.

Only, who stopped?! For one thing, I rarely walked past them at all. At the bottom of the steps, I usually took the path leading to my car so that I could drive off to do whatever it was that I was doing. But now, with fewer errands and a very limited number of places to go, I have been leaving my apartment on foot more frequently which takes me past the roses.

Perhaps it's due to the shrinking of my observable world or the fact that I have more time, but these beautiful flowers and even the more "pedestrian" plants in our front garden are absorbing much more of my attention and appreciation.

As to people, I am an avid "people person." Two of my greatest pleasures are entertaining guests at my Shabbat table or sitting and chatting in a restaurant across from a friend or family member. But I also have a wandering eye. I have always found it difficult to focus entirely on the person in front of me, partly because I am easily distracted.

These days, when I am fortunate enough to be able to look at someone's face, masked or otherwise, I am deriving great pleasure from it. I am willing to settle for a screen face, but I much prefer people to pixels.

But one of the most interesting "views" on Planet Corona is the view of *Olam Habah*, The World to Come, which is observable, even if only as a "peek." Just as Shabbat is described as being a taste—perhaps 1/60th—of Olam Habah, we have access to that on Planet Corona.

First of all, as with Shabbat, we are experiencing more quiet, fewer disturbances, more family time, and more time for reflection (unless we choose to spend every waking hour on Netflix!). Getting back to the basics of life and the joys of simplicity have opened our eyes, minds, and hearts.

One of the most fascinating glimpses into the Next World that we have here on Planet Corona is the "Upside-Down World" (*olam hafuch*) that is described in Bava Batra 10 in the following aggada (parable) concerning Joseph, the son of R. Yehoshua.

> He had been ill and fell into a trance. [After he recovered] his father said to him: "What vision did you have?" He replied, "I saw a world upside down, the upper below and the lower above." [His father] said to him, "You saw a well-regulated world."

Rashi explains the meaning thus: "'The upper' refers to the wealthy who in this world are exalted. There (in the Next World) they are lowly. 'The lower' refers to the poor who are lowly in our world. There they are exalted."

Our "Upside-Down World," aka Planet Corona, appeared shortly before or after the holiday of Purim whose mantra is "*Ve'nahafoch hu*" "It (everything) was overturned," i.e., turned upside-down. How appropriate. So many things here are opposite to how they appeared BC (before corona).

We thought (as did they) that big entities ruled the world: big business, big governments, big (i.e., wealthy and/or famous) people. Corona revealed that *all of those* could be brought to a standstill by an extremely tiny virus that was originally carried by a single individual.

In his book *A Short History of Nearly Everything*, Bill Bryson ends the section which deals with microbes, bacteria, and viruses with these words: "The world belongs to the very small – and it has done for a very long time." Who would have believed?!

So, let's turn for a moment to the "important," and extraordinarily well-paid personalities of our BC world. Rock stars, sports stars, and media personalities earn very large (obscenely large?) salaries, while teachers are among the poorest-paid professionals in many First World countries. Michael Jordan, for example "is worth" (even that very term is highly offensive) $2.5 *billion*!

Yet here on Planet Corona, who are we missing the most? Are we wondering when we will get to see our next basketball game (well, of course, some of us are!), or rather, when will we be able to send our children back to school? Harvard doesn't know at the moment if it will be able to open next year other than virtually.

There was a very charming cartoon I saw years ago that portrayed teachers riding in limos and sports stars on tricycles, with a caption suggesting that that is the way things would be in "a fair world" (the Next World?)

Right now, rock concerts are silenced, movies are on hold, large sports events have to be re-scheduled, but what the world really cares about are jobs, families, health, education, and caring for the vulnerable. Also, toilet paper! But Broadway is silent as is Madison Square Garden, Yankee Stadium isn't opening and yet… the world appears not to miss them terribly.

The "heroes" of our day are those in the worlds of medicine and medical research as well as the bus drivers, grocery workers, trash collectors, street cleaners, etc. What a glimpse we are getting of what's truly important in our lives!

In truth, the *real* "upside-down world" is the one we inhabited *before* we arrived on Planet Corona. There were more choices, but less satisfaction; more activity, but also more boredom; too much food, but too little good nutrition; lots of (Facebook) "friends," but precious little companionship.

If our eyes have been opened, let us not forget what we have seen while on this planet. Perhaps we can maintain some of Planet Corona's visions and build a better world with our new blueprints.

May 5, 2020

The Corona Port Duty-Free Shop

One day, we will indeed leave Planet Corona and, hopefully, for "good!" By that I mean, not only "never to return" but also that we hope to be going to a better place, or even a "*bettered*" place. In any event, there is a law here on Corona that stands in opposition to the adage "You can't take it with you." Here the rule is "You *must* take it with you!"

This refers to the manner in which people depart from Planet Corona. When you leave, you will be taken to the spaceship (well, of course! How else would you expect to perform interplanetary travel?). While you are waiting at the spaceport, you will have to pass through the Duty-Free/Souvenir shop. Now, for an Israeli this is a no-brainer. Duty free shopping is seen by Israelis as being one of the main purposes of international travel.

But here there are a few important differences from the airport shopping we are accustomed to. For one thing, you *must* visit the shop. No exceptions. Another difference is that you are also obligated to purchase at least one item, although you may buy several. The last difference is that all of your purchases are not only duty free, they are also totally cost free (except for the trillion or so dollars that being on Corona has cost globally. So far).

You see, the Coronese government doesn't want you ever to forget your "visit" to its planet. And so it insists that you take something with you that will remind you of this place and of your experience here. Now, since you may not be a very quick decision maker, it's probably a good idea to plan in advance what it is that you wish to take with you.

(Of course, the one thing that you must *not* take with you is the virus or you will be on a round-trip flight which, judging by the way we are rushing the return to normal, appears to be a distinct possibility!)

You might be interested in purchasing a mask or pair of latex gloves. Those take up little space in your baggage and they might be useful in reminding you of the improved hygiene habits you hopefully picked up on Planet Corona (which were preferable to "picking up" the virus!). Unless we are studying to be surgeons, I believe that most of us will decidedly prefer to forego the fashion statement of the mask and glove.

Perhaps you might wish to pick up some earplugs which, besides helping you during the actual flight, will remind you of the relative quiet that prevailed on the planet for much of the time that you were there. You may want to introduce a little more quiet into your life to make room for thinking, meditation, or a pleasant uninterrupted conversation. Turning down the volume has been one of the perks of being here.

There's an excellent selection of *siddurim** in the shops. Some of us have discovered that our prayers have become much more meaningful while we've been on Planet Corona. Studies have shown that many people, of all religions, have found that their connection to God has been strengthened by this experience. Having a new siddur to remind you of that may help keep you from slipping back into old habits of *lip service* rather than *heart service*.

In the electronics section of the duty-free shop you will find a selection of unusual devices. There are smart phones, computers, tablets that have a built-in daily time limit. They automatically shut down each day after a very few hours of use. They are a sort of "going away" present that you receive from the good people of Planet Corona.

You've spent enormous amounts of time on your devices while you've been here doing Zoom, Netflix, games, videos, and even going to school. Now is the time to relish real face-to-face communication. The pixels and images were necessary on Planet Corona. Perhaps even sanity-saving. But we can now proceed to "the real thing." Friend-to-friend, grandparent-to-grandchild, teacher-to-student, face-to-face. Not pixels, but people. Real people.

The shops in the spaceport are well-stocked with a large variety of items. There are bookshelves where you can pick up a new volume to read now that you've begun to read more while you had extra time.

There are weights and exercise videos for those who started an exercise program. (While there aren't any weight restrictions on your luggage, you can't get a treadmill on the ship. For that you'll have to wait until you get back. Just don't end up using the treadmill as a place to drape the clothes you can't fit into your closet!)

And there is a section of very attractive notebooks in which you can write down the better behaviors and acts of chesed you intend to pursue when you get "back home." Each notebook comes with an instruction booklet setting out how to best implement your good intentions and resolutions. The booklet is well worth reading.

Even before you leave for the spaceport, you might decide to downsize your own "stuff." By now, you have probably discovered that you don't need all that you have in your closets, cupboards, and drawers. If so, you may want to trade in your huge luggage for smaller, easier-to-travel-with baggage. I'm sure that on Planet Corona there are places you can donate whatever you decide to leave behind.

Traveling light as we go through life keeps us from being weighed down by belongings. "More belongings, more worry."* Previously, we spent so much time in acquiring that we had far too little time for enjoying. If there's anything we've learned on this planet, it's that the things we miss the most are those things that carry no price tag and which can't be found in a shop.

I'm not sure when we will get to the spaceport. Some people, I understand, are there already, even though the flight has not yet been scheduled. I hope they've brought camping-out equipment. In any case, the shops in the spaceport won't open until flights are rescheduled.

Others are beginning to pack, but aren't in any particular rush. They assume they'll receive enough notice so as not to miss the flight.

The rest of us are just waiting, perhaps making up our shopping list of what, indeed, we want to take away from this experience. Because you really have to "take it with you" or else you might indeed forget. And that would be a terrible, terrible waste.

* Prayerbooks.
** Hillel the Elder, Ethics of the Fathers 2:7.

May 6, 2020

Reality Check: Part 1

On Planet Corona, we are beginning to see (we hope) a light at the end of the tunnel. In fact, there are those who are running through the tunnel to meet the light. Let's hope that it's not the light of an oncoming train!

However, many of us are acting decidedly more cautiously. We are maintaining the "new normal" until we have very good evidence that it is now appropriate to leave Planet Corona for Planet Earth.

In my own life, I am a little concerned that my very dear husband is likely to behave like the groundhog in Punxsutawney, Pa.! When he pokes his head out of our apartment when the "all clear" sounds, I fear he will be so startled by his own shadow he will quickly withdraw. Dragging me with him. For the next year or so!

Whatever our approach to the coming "*geula*," redemption, we are *all* still living on Planet Corona, and are in different stages of our sojourn here depending where on the planet we are situated. That means that our lives are still very different from what we were once (eons ago) used to. And these differences have been uncomfortable, disorienting, and even frightening. I have read that many psychologists predict a large rise in cases of PTSD in the future, particularly among children.

I am not for the moment addressing this letter to the people who were or are still, unfortunately, afflicted by illness. And I am certainly not writing this to those who have tragically lost loved ones during this crisis. To them goes my deep sympathy and, where relevant, a sound "*refuah sheleima*."*

However, as to the rest of us, I believe that a reality check is in order. Yes, we are at the very least inconvenienced, and perhaps even frightened, worried, "climbing the walls," or even facing serious difficulties of various kinds. But I think we still need to look at the big picture, at least as it pertains to most of us.

And, what better means for a reality check than the morning prayers with which we begin the day. After all, they are the framework of gratitude which forms our proper approach to the miraculous lives Hashem has bestowed upon us. So the question we might pose is: Are they still totally relevant? We will review them one by one:

1: *Asher natan le'shechvi bina le'havchin bein yom u'vein layla*
"Who gives the rooster (heart) understanding to distinguish day from night"

One can interpret this literally, thanking Hashem for creating the world with fascinating elements such as the fact that roosters have a built-in mechanism that allows them to be natural alarm clocks. In fact, during this crisis natural phenomena are proceeding quite well, thank you very much. Some are even in an improved state. Have you seen the photos of the much improved air quality of major world cities? Or the one of the kangaroo hopping gaily through the empty streets of Adelaide?

And, if you adopt the more common interpretation that it is the human [heart's] ability to distinguish we see that it is in our hands to differentiate between night and day, between good choices and poor choices, and between inconveniences and tragedies.

We are familiar with the serenity prayer in which we ask " To accept the things I cannot change; Courage to change the things I can; And wisdom to know the difference." We still can exercise our wisdom to know the difference.

2: *She'lo asani goy*
"Who has not made me a heathen"

This may also have several possible interpretations. We can certainly be grateful for being in Israel during this crisis since we have been doing comparatively well to this point. Additionally, for many of us, our *emuna*, our faith in Hashem, has definitely helped sustain us and continues to do so.

3: *She'lo asani aved*
"Who has not made me a slave"

While we are undoubtedly feeling the limitations of our freedom, there are two examples of curtailed freedom that are far more extreme. In his book, *Responsa from the Holocaust*, Rabbi Ephraim Oshry includes a question as to whether a Jew in the ghetto could honestly say this prayer in the morning, considering how enslaved to Nazi whims he was. The answer was that in the deepest sense of freedom, the freedom of the mind, the Jews remained free and should continue to say this prayer.

The other example is that of Natan Sharansky, who underwent years of the most brutal of solitary confinements, including many months of being forced to stand and stare at a wall day after day. Yet, he says that he kept his thoughts and spirit free by playing chess games in his mind and by making irreverent remarks to his tormentors to show that he retained freedom of his own expression.

We are not at all in the dire straits, freedom-wise, of these two examples. We have freedom to leave our homes, and even if there are restrictions, we still have access to fresh air, to exercise, and to attending to necessities.

But even at more restricted points, we have always retained our freedom of thought, of imagination, of practicing our religious rituals (even if in a somewhat altered way). Some of us have found that by having a little less freedom of going out, we've found much greater freedom and opportunity to go within.

In my next letter I hope to continue with this "reality check." However, in the meantime, I would like to add another thought, particularly important I believe at this time of loosening restrictions. This idea also comes from our prayers. The second paragraph of the *Shema* begins with the following words:

> *Ve'haya* im *tishme'u el mitzvotai asher anochi metzaveh etchem hayom...*
> "*If* you indeed heed My commandments with which I charge you today..."

The section goes on to describe the rewards that will ensue *if* Jews keep Hashem's commandments. But not if they *don't* do so. In that case, the same section delineates the evil that will follow if we "go astray."

The analogy to our situation, I think, is that we are loosening restrictions and we hope that this will not trigger a resurgence of sickness. Hopefully, it will not do so, but that is true *only* if the rules are followed.

We must continue social distancing, wearing masks, and take care in what and whom we touch. At this point we can see our friends and family. But at this point, no hugs and no handshakes. Otherwise the safe shift to "normal" will turn into a resumption of suffering and restrictions.

Stay safe and healthy.

* Complete recovery.

May 10, 2020

A Planet Corona Shabbat

Shavua Tov. Another Planet Corona Shabbat. Another opportunity to refresh and restart and refocus. A humorous thought that's going around is "Now there are only two days in the week. Shabbat and not-Shabbat." Indeed, the other days of the week really seem to melt together during this period but, blessedly, Shabbat is still distinguishable from the rest. I may never have appreciated it more.

It's been a long time since either my husband or I worked full-time (since he's an academic, arguably he *never* worked full time!) but we still have our weekday lives and our Shabbat lives. Though this crisis has made many of us feel somewhat enclosed and enslaved, on Shabbat we are always free.

That idea appears to be counter-intuitive because so often the accent on the laws of Shabbat seems to be on all the don'ts. But it is in fact within those forbidden areas that we find true choice and freedom. Rabbi Jonathan Sacks writes, "Freedom does not mean *not* working. It means the ability to *stop* working. Shabbat is the first taste of freedom."

In the repetition of the *Aseret Hadibrot* (the Ten Commandments), where the command is to "Observe" (*Shemor*) the Shabbat, the reason given is that Hashem redeemed us from our slavery in Egypt.

The term "Observe" or *Shemor* connects to the negative commandments, the don'ts, and that is related to our having been slaves. So what we don't do, what we are both forbidden from doing but also exempt from doing, is a true expression of our redemption. That is what frees up our one day to concentrate on those important elements that we often ignore or pay lip service to during the week. Things like family, meaningful prayer, unhurried thought, and our relationship to Hashem and to our deepest selves.

So much of what we are exposed to these days are "humorous" scenarios and descriptions of how this crisis is causing us all to fall apart. We're entertained by jokes and cartoons, maybe not so funny, about sitting around all day, in our pajamas, watching Netflix, and gaining weight. And being ready to cause severe bodily damage to family members.

A serious column that appeared in our weekend newspaper essentially said that if you are overeating, not changing your clothes, feeling depressed, at least now you have a good excuse. So, don't be hard on yourself.

While I am not at all suggesting that people *should* be hard on themselves, I wonder why so many of us seem to eagerly embrace the state of being helpless victims with a very good excuse for letting ourselves go. There is, indeed, a great deal of hardship today and the future is grey and worrying, but certainly no more so than the days of the Shoah.

Yet Viktor Frankl, the well-known psychiatrist and Holocaust survivor who wrote *Man's Search for Meaning*, famously said, "Everything can be taken from a man but one thing, the last of the human freedoms – to choose one's attitude in any given set of circumstances, to choose one's own way."

Rav Yosef Dov Soloveitchik distinguished between the man of fate and the man of destiny. The man of fate is the one who is an object, *pummeled* by the vicissitudes of life. The man of destiny is the one who takes positive action to *learn and grow* from the vicissitudes of life.

And that is the gift of a Planet Corona Shabbat. A blogger—by his own admission not an observant Jew—recently wrote that he and his family have chosen to put away the technical devices for the day of Shabbat. They decided they needed a "day of rest" from the news, cartoons, videos, movies, and Zoom classes. They determined to use technology only for being in touch with family and friends and for nothing else. He shared that it turned out to be the best day of the week.

Undoubtedly, a Planet Corona Shabbat differs significantly from the Shabbat experience we had become used to. I would never have imagined that I could survive so many Shabbatot without company. But we can embrace the changes and the differences. We can accentuate all the positive elements of our Shabbat experience. We should dress as well as we have previously done, prepare delicious foods, sing *zemirot*, even if, as a young woman told me today, you have to do it alone.

The Shabbat Queen visits Planet Corona and we don't have to keep our distance from her when she enters our home. We should greet her with all the respect that is due her and rejoice in her presence.

May 11, 2020

Reality Check: Part 2

I have to admit that I'm feeling rather discouraged at the moment. I know very well that I am still on Planet Corona and I'm likely to be here for a long time still. Perhaps a Planet Corona with some loosening of restrictions, but here nonetheless. Yet, I strongly sense that there are many out there (particularly in the Holyland section of the planet where I live) who are on their way to the spaceport for the ship bound for Earth.

There are others who appear to think that they are already on Earth once again without having had the need to leave this planet. What they don't realize is that they are actually in the Six Flags EarthWorld Park which was built by the Coronese for those visitors who miss Disneyworld. Won't they be shocked when they realize that?!?

I think we *all* need a "reality check." For the moment, however, I will continue with Part 2 of the letter I began several days ago. As you may recall we began to revisit the *Birchot Hashachar* to check if they are still relevant, or perhaps even more so, on Planet Corona. Which brings us to the fourth, and often the most controversial of the *brachot*:

4. *She'asani kirtzonoh*

"Who has made me according to His will" (women's version of the fourth blessing)

First of all, I will mostly deal with the women's version of this bracha as that's the one with which I have real familiarity. I will just comment that my sense is that during these times the women are probably *still* taking responsibility for the majority of what's going on in the home so... enough said! But, on the positive side, the "being fashioned according to Hashem's will" resonates deeply within me during these days.

I believe that women are, in general, more in tune with "being" than with "doing" than men are, and that "being" has been less impacted than "doing." Which is not to say that there have not been serious impacts on women on many levels. However, in Aramaic the word for "wife" is the same as for "home" and I think that women are typically more "at home" *in* the home and, by choice to a large degree, are more responsible for making their space "a home."

5. *Pokeach ivrim*
"Who gives sight to the blind"

Whether this bracha is interpreted literally, wherein we are thanking Hashem for allowing our vision to operate properly, or whether it is more broadly understood, I think its significance has actually been enhanced during these times. "Eyes have they, but they see not" is true of many of us much of the time. We were exposed to so much visual stimuli as we rushed about before that we often did not really *see* what we were looking at. We probably seldom even *looked* at what we were observing.

As our sphere of visual experience has contracted, the attention we are giving to that within our purview has increased. And, if we are speaking of "vision" in a more spiritual sense, being on Planet Corona has given us much more opportunity to look within ourselves and to see those closest to us in a deeper way.

6. *Malbish arumim*
"Who clothes the naked"

This bracha certainly must have grabbed your attention during these days (that is, if you *pay* attention when reciting it). Whether you are thanking Hashem for comfy pajamas with elastic waists that you wear most or all of the day (Wait! Should you really be praying in pajamas?) or if you have noticed that you really *do* have more clothing than you need, you must have noticed that the fact that you are usually adequately, even nicely, clothed has been something you've always taken for granted.

The Torah is said to have begun with an act of chesed when Hashem clothed Adam and Chava (Eve) after their sin in the Garden of Eden. And that was just one suit of clothes. How grateful we should be for the clothing, weather appropriate and even fashionable, that we've been blessed with over the years. What we choose to wear while we are shut in is entirely up to us!

7. *Matir asurim*
"Who sets captives free"

This idea was partly dealt with in the bracha "Who has not made me a slave." But being imprisoned is not the same as being a slave and perhaps is closer to what we are experiencing. Of course, our "imprisonment" is not to be compared to that of the refusenik Natan Sharansky or many others like him in our history. For we have a great amount of freedom of movement within our home and, increasingly, outside of it. Besides, our minds are always free to travel and wander, both within and without.

The poet Emily Dickinson rarely left her home in Amherst and yet wrote many exquisite, deep, and insightful poems. With our books, technology, and within our own imaginations we can travel far and wide. Many people have "covered" many thousands of miles without really broadening their horizons, while others have derived much more by exploring the world right outside their door.

8. *Zokef kefufim*
"Who raises those bowed down."

This brought to mind two associations, both of which I believe are particularly relevant today. One is the story of Mordechai who refused to bow down to Haman. In the words of the megilla, "… But Mordechai would not bow…" and the word for "bow" is in the future tense. Because we do not and will not "bow," not really. Not to tyrants or to dictatorships, not to anti-Semites nor, for that matter, to any mortal beings, ideas, or "isms." As it says in the Aleinu prayer, "For they ('the multitudes') bow to vanity and emptiness," but "We bow in worship and thank the Supreme King of Kings, the Holy One, blessed be He."

It is undeniably true that there is much to fear today on Planet Corona—the virus, growing anti-Semitism, worry over our future financial stability, our health, and great trepidation about what this world will look like PC (post-corona). But *Ein od Milvado.* Only He holds the world's future and our individual futures in His Hands. And that should allow us to stand straight, unbowed, and confident.

As Rabbi J. J. Schacter said last night on an OU Zoom forum, "I don't know what we will have to do. I just know that when the time comes, we *will* know what to do and we have the resources to do it!"

Amen.

May 12, 2020

Reality Check: Part 3

Today is Lag Ba'Omer. According to tradition, this is the day on which the terrible plague that killed Rabbi Akiva's 24,000 students ceased. Prayer on this day is exceptionally powerful. I think we can all connect the dots.

In continuing the "reality check" in which we have been reviewing the Birchot Hashachar as to their relevance at this time, we come to the ninth bracha:

9. *Rokah ha'aretz al hamayim*
"Who spreads the earth above the waters"

In his book *Rav Schwab on Prayer*, Rabbi Shimon Schwab describes this bracha as showing gratitude for the security of standing on "terra firma." He describes having experienced two earthquakes and the terrifying insecurity when the "earth moves under your feet." There are many natural laws that make our lives possible. Gravity "always" works. When I toss up a ball, it *will* come down again. There's security in knowing that. But it is Hashem who, in His kindness, makes it work that way. Natural laws have been and can be suspended by His decree. But rarely, or else a sane life would be impossible.

Today, nature has taken us by surprise. We are shocked by the havoc that can be caused by a natural occurrence like a virus. Perhaps, it's to remind us of all the elements of nature that we depend on, function with and... take for granted. Perhaps we can express our gratitude for what still works, which is most of it, and realize that all of nature is merely a servant of Hashem.

10. *She'asa li kol tzorchi*
"Who has provided me with all I need"

My mindfulness teacher Dr. Dina Wyshograd often reminds us to "accept ourselves as we are at the moment, rather than to wish, as we all do, that things should be different from the way they are." That doesn't mean that we can't hope and pray that in the future things could improve. It just means that, at the moment, everything and everyone is exactly where and how they are supposed to be at that moment. We don't understand Hashem's plan, particularly now. But He has one. That's an essential belief. Essential for me, anyway.

11. *Hameichin mitzadei gaver*
"Who makes firm the steps of man"

Once again, I am drawn to the interpretation of Rabbi Schwab who sees this bracha as the one that turns from thanking Hashem for the gifts He has bestowed upon us to an appreciation for the fact that He enables us, through the inestimable gift of Free Choice, to take those actions during the coming day that will lead us either along the correct path or paths, or not.

Not only do we have the free choice to determine the direction our lives will take, but He has given us all the tools, our hands, feet, eyes, etc., to carry out our determination.

We also have the assurance that if we wish to do good, He will help us along that path. That is so true, even today. Perhaps even more so. Because, as the challenges to our acting positively increase, we have assurance that so does Hashem's help in valuing and supporting our efforts.

12. *Ozer Yisrael bigvura*
"Who girds Israel with strength"

It is promised that we are girded, firmed, and supported. That should breed confidence and security. Our country has done well. That is not to deny the disproportionate toll on Am Yisrael elsewhere. Too many of us have been stricken with and stricken down by this deadly virus. But we are guaranteed that we have the strength to make it to the other side and to grow from our loss and pain. It's happened before. Countless times.

13. *Oter Yisrael be'tifara*
"Who crowns Israel with glory" (*tiferet*)

When it is darkest, there is greater opportunity to truly shine. When others cannot or will not meet the challenges, then those who do stand out. And when our Nation does so, either as an entity or as individuals, we bring "tiferet" to ourselves and, by extension, to Hashem. In Pirkei Avot, The Ethics of the Fathers, it says that the right path to choose is one that is "'tiferet' (honor, glory, splendor) to the one who chooses it and "tiferet" in the eyes of others.

We can choose actions that are gracious, honorable, even splendid, which will reflect on us as individuals and also as part of the Jewish People and, further, will bring "tiferet" to the Name of Hashem. Or we can choose to do otherwise. That choice is still open to all of us.

14. *Hanoten leya'ef koach*
"Who gives strength to the weary"

It has been said that "When the going gets tough, the tough get going." But it's not as if those "toughs" knew they had it in them to indeed "get going," nor did they ask for the "going" to "get tough." These are not things we wish for. A friend, who has had many serious difficulties in her life, once confided in me that in her prayers she often asks Hashem, in weariness, to please make the road smoother. But we agreed that was in the category of a *bracha le'vatala*, "a vain petition." The best she could hope for was to receive better shock absorbers! Certainly, there must have been times when your ability to survive difficulties, and to do so with grace, surprised even you. This can be one of those times.

15. *Gomel chasadim tovim le'amoh Yisrael*
"Who bestows beneficent kindnesses on His people [of] Israel"

That there is much good in our lives, there is no doubt. We see that in the morning blessings that we have reviewed here. However, there can be good that isn't sweet and doesn't even feel particularly good. Yet Hashem does, indeed, sweeten the sometimes painful events that occur "for our own good." That is the understanding of "beneficent kindnesses," i.e., beneficial corrections that are also administered with a gentled Hand.

When Joseph is sold to a caravan of traders going to Egypt, our Sages say that, very atypically, this caravan carried sweet spices rather than the malodorous goods that usually traveled that route. That was so that Joseph, who was part of a very momentous story in our history, should at least not be assaulted by terrible smells on his way. This is known as "sweetening the judgement."

These days of separation and loss are so very difficult. But, we have Zoom (two months ago I didn't even know what that was!), WhatsApp, cellphones, kind neighbors, and many sweeteners to offset some of the bitter realities of Planet Corona. And for that we must be grateful.

May 15, 2020

Growing Pains

On Planet Corona, the spiritual biologists have developed an unusual growth hormone. It promotes psychological, spiritual, and emotional development. Since it has no negative side effects, it has been introduced into the water supply, like fluoride, so that everyone is receiving it. However, it has an interesting placebo-like quality. It's only effective if you choose it to be.

As it has no side effects, those who don't wish the hormone to affect them will find that it doesn't. In truth, there are only painful side effects if the hormone is effective and it affects only those who choose to allow the growth hormone to work on them. The side effects are known as "growing pains."

And growing can indeed be painful. Stretching yourself mentally, reaching for greater spiritual heights, learning to better deal with emotions—all have great benefits. But those "exercises" are not without difficulty. There is a reality of "no pain, no gain."

Some of us actually welcome this aspect of our time on Planet Corona because it affords us an opportunity to rethink some of our ideas, reevaluate our relationships, and reconnect with our spiritual selves. Still, these are challenging stretches especially if we have been unused to them.

Let's face it. Being lazy is an all-too-common human trait. At least the kind of laziness that holds you back from trying to be the best "you" that you are capable of being.

There is an oft-told story of Rav Zusha of Hanipol which describes the following scene:

> When Rav Zusha was on his deathbed, his students found him in uncontrollable tears. They tried to comfort him by telling him that he was almost as wise as Moses and as kind as Abraham, so he was sure to be judged positively in Heaven. He replied, "When I get to Heaven, I will not be asked 'Why weren't you like Moses?' or 'Why weren't you like Abraham?' for I will be able to answer, 'I was not created with the potential of either a Moses or an Abraham. However, the question that I fear is, 'But, Rav Zusha, why weren't you like Zusha? Why did you not fully live up to your own potential?' That is the question that I fear. And for that question, I have no answer."

The wake-up call that signaled our voyage to Planet Corona is similar to the sound of the shofar blowing during the month of Elul. Maimonides describes it as an alarm whose purpose is to awaken the slumberers so that they can repent. Many of us go through life half-asleep, doing what we've always done, thinking what we've always thought, behaving in habitual ways. Now, we've been shaken to our very foundations.

We've been given this chance to look at ourselves, our country, our world and ask the questions that need to be asked both personally and globally. Are we traveling along a positive and productive path? Have we done all we can to improve our environment, human interactions, relationship to God? Are we even *trying* to improve so that tomorrow is a better day than today?

It has occurred to me that here on Planet Corona, what we miss most are our former diversions. All the busyness that allowed us, on Planet Earth, to ignore the most important issues. So we've been filling our time with more and more videos, movies, cartoons, clips. Just not to allow the Corona growth hormone to have an effect on us. And when we do think, it's along the lines of "What shall I do?" rather than "Who can I be?" It could be laziness. It could also be fear. As Marianne Williamson wrote in *A Return to Love*:

> Our deepest fear is not that we are inadequate. Our deepest fear is that we are powerful beyond measure. It is our light, not our darkness that most frightens us. We ask ourselves, "Who am I to be brilliant, gorgeous, talented, fabulous?" Actually, who are you not to be? You are a child of God. Your playing small does not serve the world. There is nothing enlightened about shrinking so that other people won't feel insecure around you. We are all meant to shine, as children do. We were born to make manifest the glory of God that is within us. It's not just in some of us; it's in everyone. And as we let our own light shine, we unconsciously give other people permission to do the same. As we are liberated from our own fear, our presence automatically liberates others.

We are all permeated with the Planet Corona growth hormone. Don't forget that it's in our water supply. When we leave the planet we will have the opportunity to purchase a limited amount to take back with us to Earth. It will just be more expensive.

The only question is, are we willing to let it take effect within us? Can we overcome the laziness that causes us to balk at the challenges to our being better citizens, better friends, better people than we were when we arrived? Because, one day we may also be faced with the question that caused Rav Zusha to weep, "Why, when I gave you the opportunity, did you not work towards being the best You that you could be?" What will you answer?

May 18, 2020

The Planet Corona Blues

It is definitely "one of those days" again on Planet Corona. Is it my imagination, or are they occurring more frequently? I find myself pacing the floors like a caged animal in an old-fashioned zoo. Any wonder that my name is Chaya (One of its meanings is an animal)? If I didn't actually *like* my apartment so much, by now I think I'd *hate* it! And consequently, I am also not happy with myself for being so ungrateful.

I *have* a pleasant apartment which has decent air-conditioning (Did I mention that it is very hot outside?), plenty of food, no bored children, and a cheerful companion, my husband Eli, who at the moment appears to be doing much better than I am.

A friend asked me today, "Are you also going stir crazy?" "Yes, I am!" I responded instantly. So, I believe that it's a propitious time for doing a personal "reality check" and "gratitude evaluation" to hopefully effect the necessary recalibration.

For one thing, today is the Zoom bat mitzva of my darling granddaughter, Shira, which is guaranteed to be as lovely as she is. I might even be grateful for the lack of tempting high calorie treats that would have been served at a live celebration.

In my tefillot this morning, I made a greater than usual attempt to pay attention to the fact that the things that I verbally *claim* to be grateful for are indeed blessings even on less-than-wonderful days on Planet Corona.

While it is, indeed, very hot outside, that itself contains a hidden blessing. It really isn't all that tempting to spend much time outside, unlike if the weather were more temperate. In fact, the weather here seems to have gone straight from February to August, making staying inside not quite the misfortune that it might be otherwise.

Some of the elements that are giving me "the blues" are the newspaper headlines of the political machinations taking place ("When will they ever learn?") and the many Israelis (as well as the inhabitants of other parts of the world) who don't seem to be taking the Covid19 restrictions seriously enough. ("Oh, when will *they* ever learn?")

But then I take a deep breath and remember that "they" (the politicians, the unmasked scoffers, the standing-too-close virus spreaders) don't run the world. No one has a clue how this crisis will continue to play out which means that *neither do I*! So, there's no sense in worrying about whatever may or may not happen.

Well, several hours have passed since I began this Letter. In that time, I've participated in Shira's delightful Zoom bat mitzva. It was beautiful and meaningful and memorable. I am so grateful to have such a special family and even if we can't at the moment hug and kiss, the love came through mutually. Because it was on Zoom, relatives in the US could also participate. So thanks for that, Hashem.

We also participated in two other virtual get-togethers which united, at least on the screen, family members who couldn't otherwise see one another. So, thanks Hashem for the technology that allows us to have face-time with friends and family even at a time such as this.

As Rabbi Jonathan Sacks pointed out recently, here the *Refuah* preceded the *Maka* (the cure preceded the plague) so that it almost appears that these technological advances came into being just for Planet Corona! Once again, thanks so much!

I know that I cannot change much of what is happening in my life and in the world. And I can choose to be out-of-sorts and a trial to those I'm in communication with, principally my husband, or I have the choice to be less reactive and more positive in my approach to events on this planet.

Again, who can impart greater wisdom than Dr. Viktor Frankl, whose Holocaust experiences make him perhaps the authority on dealing with difficulties and tragedy: "Between stimulus and response there is a space. In that space is our power to choose our response. In our response lies our growth and our freedom."

I can see that I may need some help in learning how to negotiate the choppy waters of Planet Corona. Perhaps I'll visit the Office of Energy Conservation one day this week. I understand they can be very helpful. I'll gladly share with you, my fellow inhabitants of Planet Corona, any useful ideas and practices I pick up there. In the meantime, stay healthy, and even happy.

May 19, 2020

My Visit to the DEC

Despite the extreme heat of the day, I determined to visit the Department of Energy Conservation (DEC) of Planet Corona. Previously, I had learned that it was a governmental department that helped citizens with techniques for saving all sorts of energy—physical, spiritual, and emotional—besides those for conserving energy resources.

I ventured out minus a mask, as the new rule, at least for the next four days, is that masks are not required out-of-doors because of the heat. I imagine that people have been dropping like flies, not due to Covid-19, but because of the heat-plus-mask combination.

The DEC is located in one of the main government buildings which also meant that it was difficult to find the exact department I was looking for. I finally found the offices of the DEC, which consisted of a few smallish but cheerful-looking rooms. On the waiting-room walls were attractive posters with messages such as:

> "Yesterday is history, tomorrow is a mystery, today is a gift of God, which is why we call it the present."
> "God, grant me the serenity to accept the things I cannot change, the courage to change the things I can, and the wisdom to know the difference."
> "Worry is like a rocking chair: it gives you something to do but never gets you anywhere."

Since I was the only visitor waiting to be seen, I barely had time to read the posters before I was called into one of the rooms to meet with the DEC representative. She was a pleasant-looking young woman whose name-tag identified her as Emuna Bitchoni.* She smiled as she asked me to take a seat and inquired in what way she could help.

Before beginning my personal inquiries, I commented on the rather small quarters that the DEC occupied. "I would imagine," I said, "that *many* people might need some help dealing with the energy-sapping emotional and physical challenges of the present crisis?"

"You would think so, wouldn't you?" she replied with a sigh. "In fact, we had larger quarters initially, expecting a flood of people searching for well-researched and sensible solutions for the challenges of these times. However, we soon discovered that most people seemed to prefer doom-and-gloom to positive techniques."

"So, Miss Bitchoni ("Call me Emuna," she insisted), which department deals with *those* people," I asked.

"That would be the Department of Communications and Media (DCM)," she responded. "They have an entire floor of offices presently. They appear to be the experts in doom-and-gloom."

With a wistful look, Emuna sighed, "I originally applied for a position there. I think they took one look at my name and didn't even read my resume. "But," she hurriedly added, "what can I do to help you?"

So I proceeded with the tale of my woes. "I find myself worrying a lot about what's happening, but more about what's going to be. When will it be over? What will everything look like when it's over?"

"Ah," she said, "for that you would need to visit our Department of Prophetic Pronouncements (DPP)." Seeing my incredulous look, she added with a smile, "No, no, that was just a joke. A good laugh is always such a useful technique. No, there is no such department, although there are several "prophets of doom" over at DCM.

"But, seriously," she continued, "you were speaking of your tendency to worry, which is so common, especially these days. Did you notice our posters outside?"

"Yes, I did," I replied.

"Well, we have another one that's going up this afternoon," she said. "It says: '*Worry never robs tomorrow of its sorrow, it only saps today of its joy.*' A senior member of our department has said that worry is not at all 'cost-effective.' Because when you worry, one of two things is going to happen. Either what you worry about will never come to pass, which is what usually happens, meaning that you've worried at least once for nothing.

"Or it *might* come to pass," she continued, "in which case you've had the negative experience twice, once in anticipation and once in reality. Which also means that you've had one *extra* negative bout. It just doesn't make any sense either way."

"I hear you," I quickly replied. "But you make it sound as if I have a choice in the matter. I don't *want* to worry. I just do!"

"No," she insisted stubbornly (No more Miss Nice Guy?) "You do have a choice! I'm sure you've read Dr. Viktor Frankl's quote about the space between stimulus and response where we have the power to choose."

"Actually," I admitted, "I even wrote about that idea. Perhaps I really should read what I write!"

"That's a good idea," she laughed. "Anything else?"

"Well, yes," I answered. "I also find myself getting angry at people who are not obeying the rules, thereby endangering the rest of us. It's so selfish and thoughtless!"

"I really do hear that," she agreed. "We refer to them as TWERPs, **T**houghtless and **W**itless **E**ndangerers of the **R**esident **P**opulace. Still, there probably isn't anything you can do about them. So, it amounts to an unnecessary waste of energy, which, like worry, saps the physical, emotional, and spiritual resources needed for the real challenges that you can actually do something about."

"I think I get the message," I smiled. "By the way, I didn't notice your division for conserving traditional energy resources. Where would it be?"

"Oh," she said. "It's temporarily closed. For one thing, we don't expect people to come about saving electric power because we'd probably tell them to cut down on air-conditioning. In which case, in this brutal heat wave, they'd probably physically attack us.

"As to saving on fuel, nobody's driving or flying today so there is actually a glut of oil at the present. We have been considering mounting a bail-out for poor suffering Iran!"

In response to my look of shock, she laughingly said, "Just another joke! Don't worry."

As I got up to leave, I concluded, "Well, Emuna, you have been very helpful and pleasant. Makes me wonder if I'm really in a government office!"

She smiled and said, "Perhaps we just do things differently on Planet Corona than what you've been used to."

"Perhaps," I murmured to myself as I left the DEC. "Perhaps."

* Play on words. In Hebrew, "Believe [and] Trust [in] Me."

May 22, 2020

Yom Yerushalayim* on Planet Corona

Once again, I was in the middle of writing an entirely different letter and Yom Yerushalayim intervened. How could I possibly allow this opportunity to pass by? Sitting here in the Holy City in the Holy Land on Planet Corona, I remind myself that there are constant and unchanging truths that a virus such as Covid-19 can never affect. Surely, we all have discovered that although so many things have changed, others have not. Or, if there has been a difference, it's been for the better.

Many have found that our tefillot are less hurried and more sincere and meaningful. Hopefully, our sympathy for and empathy with others has increased. For one thing, I have found that my level of gratitude for the "simple" things of life has grown considerably. Yesterday, I received the following:

> A story has been circulating about a 93-year-old man who recovered from corona. The hospital clerk told him he had to pay $5,000 out-of-pocket for the use of the ventilator for one day in the hospital.
>
> The old man began to cry.
>
> The people around him tried to reassure him. "Don't worry, everything will be fine. It's only money."
>
> The elderly man then said, "I'm not crying because of the money I have to pay. I can afford it. I'm crying because I just realized that I have been breathing God's air for 93 years and I never paid a penny for it. If it costs over $5,000 to use the air from the ventilator for one day, how much do I owe God for 93 years of air—and I never even thanked him once!"

Just yesterday I, too, had noticed the difference between breathing with a mask and without it. Particularly in this hot weather, the difference was "breath-taking." Yet, had I ever thanked Hashem for being able to breathe unhindered before, or for breathing at all? We all know the answer.

I remember the time when I knew that in Israel there was a place known as the Wailing Wall where Jews could not go. That had been the case for all the years that I had lived. My future husband, Eli, had been in Jerusalem in September 1966 and had climbed up to the roof of Notre Dame just outside the Old City walls, which was the one place a Jew could go to look over the walls into the Old City. Not to actually see anything particularly significant, but just to look and hope.

He remembers thinking to himself wistfully, "I wonder if I will live long enough to actually be able to enter into that walled city." Nine months later, he was there!

Fifty-three years ago, I was a freshman at Stern College. In the weeks leading to the war, we were all in turmoil, wondering what would result from the daily threats made by the Arab countries. The Straits of Tiran had been closed. Because so many Israeli men had been ordered to report for duty, there was a shortage of workers in agriculture and in other areas. So, many people volunteered to fly to Israel and help cover the labor shortage. Some of my friends had gone. I, too, had commenced procedures for volunteering when the outbreak of the war intervened.

In the early days of the war, there was no news out of Israel for security reasons. However, the Arab countries were broadcasting their "triumphs" over the Israeli army and we were in terror. Of course, it was all lies and bravado, but we didn't know that then.

Each day we and thousands of others crowded into Dag Hammarskjold Plaza across from the UN where loudspeakers had been set up blaring the ongoing news of the war from WINS.

On the 28 of Iyar, we were standing in the plaza as the news of the conquest of the Old City was being broadcast. We stood in shocked amazement and in joy. At the end of the newscast, the reporter signed off, "This is Jay Bushinsky, reporting from an undivided Jerusalem!" To this day, those words give me goosebumps.

Some truths are unchanging and have only become more powerful even during this crisis. Or perhaps even stand out in greater relief because there are fewer distractions. One of these is that Yerushalayim belongs forever to the Jewish people.

We write about it, sing its songs, learn the Torah that comes out of Zion, study its history, and delight in the archaeological finds that support our story and our claim.

It is a constant theme in all our prayers and our liturgy. It is in our thoughts and on our lips at every important occasion; every wedding, Pesach Seder, during the Yamim Noraim (the High Holidays), and every day.

From the very first exile, we vowed that if we ever forgot Yerushalayim, we would call down curses upon ourselves for having had the audacity to forget the unforgettable. "*Im eshkachaych Yerushalayim.*"**

We yearned and were returned. And not just to Yerushalayim and the Kotel (the Wailing Wall). But, also to Rachel's Tomb, Hebron, Shilo, the Golan Heights, and so much more.

Perhaps we've grown so used to this that we've forgotten to be adequately grateful. As if it is even possible to be "adequately grateful"! Because we are on Planet Corona, many of us cannot experience these wondrous places other than virtually.

But we can remind ourselves that they will be there waiting for us when we return. That has not changed. That will never change. For that we must be eternally grateful. Today and every day. Shabbat Shalom and *Yom Yerushalayim sameach*!

* Jerusalem Day.
** If I [would] forget thee, O Jerusalem.

May 26, 2020

Packing to Leave: Part 1

I'm "beginning to consider thinking" about packing to leave Planet Corona. Perhaps that conveys the vagueness of my intentions. I am painfully aware that many people are not only packed but are also under the impression that they have left already. Perhaps they are correct, but there is good reason to question it. In which case, they have probably landed on Planet Denial, which is actually an even less pleasant planet in the system. Most of the unpleasantness results from the shock of realizing that what looks like Home... isn't.

Of course, it is possible that they actually *have* made it Back Home which is why I am "beginning to consider thinking" about leaving and commencing to pack. My husband has not even reached *that* point. He believes that departure is a very long way off. Perhaps. But I hope not.

However, it's not only the health concerns that keep me from packing with great enthusiasm in breathless anticipation. There are actually some aspects of the life here that the two of us have grown to appreciate. I've heard a similar reluctance from other people. They, too, have discovered some pleasant features of this planet that they are loath to leave behind.

But, of course, the truth is that you actually can take many of those elements with you. It's like a cutting from a treasured plant that you wrap carefully in order to transplant it wherever it is you are going. Naturally, you need to choose the cutting carefully and tend it well after it's been replanted so that it thrives. But, it not only can be done, it ought to be done. What a shame to leave behind the treasures that have been discovered on Planet Corona when they can be taken with you.

Whether it's better tefillot, closer family relationships, a new talent that you've found within you, an increased appreciation for the blessings in your life, or a deeper sense of gratitude in general, all these can turn your Back Home into a Better Home.

If you haven't left Planet Corona yet, or if you are not so caught up in the return trip that you don't have time for reflection, now is a good time to think of what it is that you want to transplant and how you will go about doing so.

I am saving space in my baggage for several "items." One of these is the sense of unity that I have come to feel over the last few months with those in the ever-widening ripples of my existence.

I've developed a deeper sense of closeness to family members despite the fact that I haven't been able to see them in person, or only very occasionally. Absence has most definitely made the heart grow fonder. The challenge is to retain the fondness when "absence" is no longer obligatory.

Although I see my friends less, I think of them more. I certainly miss them, but we have found ways of communicating and some of them are "keepers." For example, there is a group of friends who have known each other for 50+ years (aren't we fortunate!?). However, we don't all live in Israel. So, we have met over Zoom and it has been delightful. And, assuming that Zoom will not end with the current crisis (and I don't think we need worry about Zoom's financial state!), then this would be a practice well worth continuing.

On a deeper level, my friends have become more special to me in that I am enjoying their good times with them (several have celebrated 50th wedding anniversaries in this period) and I am concerned for their continuing good health.

In the ripples further from the center, I find my fellow Jews, Israelis, and the rest of humanity who live on the same Planet Corona that I do. We have shared so much, albeit that the closer to the center the more commonality there is.

In the restricted world that I have inhabited for the last few months, there's a certain grandeur in the fact that so much of the global population is going through many of the same challenges and, unfortunately, sorrows. But it's not so much that "misery loves company," rather it's a feeling of solidarity with much of humanity that is new to me.

But, after I've chosen this "cutting" that I wish to take with me and have wrapped it up carefully, I need to think *now* about how I will transplant it when I return. If I hesitate too long to replant it carefully, it may not survive. And that would be a tragedy after all the time that I've spent developing and nurturing it on Planet Corona.

So, I will be thinking during these days about steps that I will commit to taking when I get "Back Home" to make it the "Best Home" that I can.

May 28, 2020

Packing Postponed—Chag Sameach

As I mentioned before, I haven't actually begun packing. However, as tonight is Shavuot I'm not even going to think about it until after the holiday. Therefore, I am postponing my "Packing to Leave: Part 2." Today is devoted to preparing for Shavuot, both physically and spiritually.

For one thing, I am reflecting on this year's Sefirat Ha'Omer,* which was unlike any other in the history of the world! Did we just "count the days" or did we "make the days count?" That is certainly the deep meaning of the original 49-day march from Egypt to *Kabbalat HaTorah.*** The Jews traveled physically to the base of Mount Sinai. But spiritually, they went from nearly the lowest level of degradation to the most sublime of heights.

Every year, we are meant to replicate their spiritual journey within our own lives. But, this year, having traveled to Planet Corona even before Pesach, we have been afforded an unprecedented opportunity to rise spiritually in a much deeper way.

There are two thoughts connected to Shavuot that I've been thinking about recently that also connect to our situation here on

Planet Corona. The first is related to the word *"vayichan"* (and *he* camped) which is used when the People of Israel arrived at the foot of Mount Sinai preparatory to receiving the Torah.

In every other instance, in relating the travels of the nation, it says *"vayis'u"* (and *they* traveled) and *"va'yachanu"* (and *they* encamped). Only in the instance at Har Sinai does it say *"vay-is'u,"* in the plural, followed by *"vayichan,"* in the singular. The Midrash comments, *"Ke'ish echad, b'lev echad"* (As one person with one heart), attesting to the unity that the Jews felt at that moment before Revelation.

We are a stubborn, argumentative, opinionated people. But "for one brief shining moment" we were united and in that mode Hashem spoke to us. Particularly in these times, many of us feel an increased sense of unity with other Jews and, for that matter, with all of humankind.

But I'd like to suggest another potential way to view the use of the singular in the word *"vayichan."* While we were, indeed, a unified nation at Mount Sinai, we were at the same time millions of single and singular humans, each connecting to *Hakadosh Baruch Hu*, the Holy One, Blessed Be He, in an individual and unique way. We might even say that on that day Hashem had a personal meeting with each one of us (our *neshamot* having been there, too).

Just as we can say, according to the Kotsker Rebbe, *"Bishvili nivra ha'olam"* (the world was created for *me* as an individual), so we can, perhaps, say that the Torah was given to *me* as an individual. In these days, when so many communal activities of prayer and study are inaccessible other than by Zoom and other electronic media, we still need to know that we, even on our own, can connect to Hashem through prayer and learning. It will be *different*. But it need not be *less*.

The second idea has to do with the concept of leadership, and is derived from the section in Masechet Brachot that deals with the Giving of the Torah as it relates to the aftermath of the Sin of the Golden Calf (Brachot 32a):

> It is stated: "*And the Lord said to Moses: Go and descend,* for your people whom you have lifted out of the land of Egypt have been corrupted" (Exodus 32:7). *What is* the meaning of "*go and descend*"? *Rabbi Elazar said: The Holy One, Blessed be He, said to Moses: Moses, descend from your greatness. Isn't it only for the sake of Israel,* so that you may serve as an emissary, *that I granted you prominence; and now that Israel has sinned, why do I need you?* There is no need for an emissary. *Immediately, Moses' strength waned, and he was powerless to speak* in defense of Israel. *And once* God *said* to Moses: "*Leave Me be, that I may destroy them*" (Deuteronomy 9:14), *Moses said* to himself: If God is telling me to let Him be, it must be because *this matter is dependent upon me. Immediately Moses stood and was strengthened in prayer, and asked* that God have *mercy* on the nation of Israel and forgive them for their transgression.

The key, and somewhat astonishing, idea is that to Hashem, Moshe *only* merited prominence insofar as he served the People of Israel. But now that the Jews were about to be wiped out because of sin "…*why do I need you?*" The message being that the leader is a servant of the people and an emissary of Hashem.

It is not about his personal stature, and never about his own aggrandizement. It is always and ever about service to those he leads. A leader, in whatever position he holds, does what he must and what he can for his people. First, last, and always.

We see that quality in the couple that "gave birth" to Israel's monarchy, Ruth and Boaz. In her Megilla (Scroll), we see Ruth as the selfless daughter-in-law who will not abandon Naomi and sustains her when they return to Bethlehem. Although a princess by birth, she volunteers to reap alongside the poor in order to provide food for the two of them.

She then agrees to marry a man much older than her in order that "the name of the deceased (her husband Machlon, son of Naomi) not be cut off from among his brethren." And when she has a child, her first, she does not appear to mind when the local women cry out, "A son has been born to *Naomi*!"

Even then, Ruth is willing to serve, even without recognition. Note, of course, that in the end *she* is known as "The Mother of Royalty" and her megilla has been read and studied for millennia!

Boaz, too, serves as a counterpoint to the other Bethlehem leader, Elimelech, husband of Naomi, who abandoned his people during a famine to avoid leading and aiding them through a crisis. Even worse, he relocates to Moav, a nation infamous to us for its ingratitude and self-centeredness.

Boaz, in contradistinction, helps sustain his people, is generous to Naomi and Ruth and, in the end, serves as the redeemer of Elimelech's abandoned property and of Machlon's and Naomi's lost hopes for a future.

And, of course, from Boaz and Ruth descends David, the epitome of the King of Israel, referred to always as "the servant of Hashem" who is also the protector and leader of the people from the day that he kills Goliath and fights the Philistines, until he begins to gather the materials for the building of the Beit Hamikdash. From David will come the Messiah who will ultimately redeem Hashem's people for Eternity.

So, where are *our* leaders in this crisis? Well, they are neither as woefully incompetent as some would have it, nor are they as wise and selfless as they might be. But then, we are a people not easily led. Even the best leaders have always had their detractors, going back to Moses and David, as well as others.

Of course, in totally unprecedented times such as these we see that even our best minds are stymied. Still, if there is a leadership vacuum, we can and must be our own leaders. Not having a leader to follow is not an excuse for aimless wandering and problematic behavior.

We have many sources of inspiration, wisdom, and leadership from the wisdom of the past and the present. And, within each of us, is the Tzelem Elokim which can help direct and lead us in a time of crisis and confusion.

As Hillel the Elder said, *Bamakom she'eyn ish, hishtadeil lihyot ish*, "In the place where there is no man, strive to be a man." Where leadership is lacking, provide it for yourself. You have it in you!

* The ritual counting of the 49 days between Pesach and Shavuot.
** Receiving the Torah.

Chapter Four

June 2020

June 1, 2020

The Department of MCECM

Yesterday was "one of those days." Again. I know that I have no gift of prophecy, but in an earlier letter I expressed a concern that many of my fellow inhabitants on Planet Corona were already packing and leaving for Home.

My fear was that rather than ending up on Planet Earth, they would be waylaid on Planet Denial, a parallel planet to Planet Corona, where they would be in for a rude awakening. It seems that fear is unfortunately materializing.

That realization, combined with several other factors, propelled me into a sort of tailspin. In an attempt to emerge from this "funk," I determined to visit the government offices of Planet Corona once more as my last visit had been helpful. Hoping that I might learn how to better manage my physical and emotional environment, I decided to see what the Department of "Mini-Climate and Environment Control and Management" (MCECM) might offer in the way of help.

Entering the suite of offices for the MCECM, I noticed two directional signs. One said, "Managing Your Physical Space" and pointed left, while the other pointed right towards "Managing Your Emotional Space." I decided to go left first as I have been experiencing a need for a change of scenery lately. I was immediately called into an office occupied by a cheerful young man who introduced himself as "Rock" Lobabayit.*

"Actually, my name is Reuven. But I thought that Rock sounds more like American and more, like cool, no?" Not wishing to deflate his mood, I just nodded.

"How can I help you?" he began. "Do you feel like you want to be in places not like your own house?"

I told him that I was used to traveling and that I was, in fact, feeling a bit bored by my all-too-familiar surroundings.

"No problem," he assured me. "We have special packages that will turn your apartment into an exotic travel destination."

I looked at him skeptically, but he continued: "Let's say you wish you were on a beautiful sunny island. We have the Hawaii Holiday Combo. There are huge posters with tropical scenes for your walls. The package includes a large bag of sand for your bathroom floor. You fill the tub with warm water and put in the blue tint that's enclosed. We suggest turning on your apartment heat, spreading the colorful bath towel we provide on the sandy floor. You might want to add a picnic lunch. We recommend sprinkling a little of the sand on the food for more authenticity."

I quickly broke in and told Rock that that wasn't exactly what I had in mind. He hurried on with "OK. No islands. How about the Antarctica Escapade. Everyone's going there these days. So, this particular package comes with a mini snow-making machine, posters of Antarctica, and a DVD of 'The Ice Age.' We recommend that you set your air-conditioner to 10° Celsius (OK. Not exactly Antarctica), bundle up and strap on the cross-country skis that are included. You should set this up in your salon so that you can at least take a few steps. Oh, and we also add a few inflatable penguins."

At that point, I realized that I had clearly taken the wrong turn when I entered the MCECM. I thanked Rock for at least attempting to be helpful, but told him that I didn't really think that destroying my present apartment (I'd need to clean for days after) would quite fit the bill.

He wished me luck and pointed me towards the other area, "Managing Your Emotional Space."

I was ushered into the office of a pleasant-looking, school-teacher'ish looking woman whose badge identified her as Tovli Babayit.** She noticed my look of bemusement and immediately said, "Yes, I am related to Rock. Rather distantly, as it happens. So, how can I help you?"

Her sympathetic manner encouraged me to really open up.

"I've been finding the most recent period here on Planet Corona to be rather stressful and even painful at times," I confessed. "Nobody seems to be following the rules. They seem to think that they are in a post-corona period, but I think they are worrisomely mistaken!"

"Yes, well, I can understand your concern and it is justified. But I am here to try to help you improve the manner in which you manage your emotional space which is limited to the things you can do something about. Tell me, is there any part of your morning ritual that distresses you?"

"Well, I do look at the news each day," I admitted. "My husband thinks I should avoid reading the latest happenings as they are usually mood-deflating, but I find myself almost compelled."

Ms. Babayit peered at me over her bifocals and tsk'ed reprovingly, "I'm sure you realize that that is your first mistake. Newspapers only ever seem to report depressing news and, as there is very little you can do about the world or even local affairs, what's the purpose of starting your day with downers? Do you have your own MONI (Minister of Necessary Information) to inform you of what you actually *need* to know?

"Yes," I replied. "My husband is able to read the news without taking it too much to heart. He passes on the information that is necessary for me to know."

"Then," she said with a smile, "it appears that you have enough MONI!"

I groaned appreciatively and she continued, "And do you always dress so monochromatically? Although tastefully, of course," she hastened to add.

I glanced down at my grey top and black skirt and answered, "Well, yes. It makes getting dressed each morning a bit simpler. No matching."

"Simpler, perhaps," she agreed, "but also not particularly cheering. Try brighter colors. They actually have been shown to lift your mood. By the way," she continued, "have you heard of Dr. Tal Ben-Shahar who taught a very popular course in Positive Psychology at Harvard before returning home to Israel several years ago?"

I replied that I had, indeed, heard of him. "Well," she said, "he has written a book entitled *Happier*, which presents techniques for improving your happiness. They include keeping a gratitude journal, exercising, meditating, and doing kind acts, amongst other ideas. It's well worth reading." I immediately made a resolution to begin reading it.

"One last idea I thought I'd share with you," she lowered her voice, almost conspiratorially. "I could get in trouble for this as one is not supposed to promote religious ideas that might offend someone. But you appear to be open to such thoughts.

"Someone wrote recently about one of God's names being Hamakom, "The Place," she confided. "It says somewhere that the Universe is not the place of Hashem, rather Hashem is The Place of the universe. So, it seems to me that anytime you feel yourself to be in the Presence of God, then you are inevitably in the Right Place, wherever it is."

As I nodded thoughtfully, she added matter-of-factly, but gently, "I hope this has helped a little to better manage your emotional, and perhaps spiritual space."

"It really has," I said with gratitude as I got up to leave. "You have given me some very useful tools. Now, I guess, it's up to me to make use of them. Stay well and healthy and thank you very much."

As I left the building feeling much lighter, I realized that the first half of my visit had given me something to laugh at and the second half had given me something to smile about. A very useful visit, indeed.

This morning, my husband asked, "Are you feeling better this morning?"

"Yes," I replied, "I believe I am!"

* Play on words. In Hebrew it means "Only not at home."
** Play on words, meaning "It's good for me at home."

June 4, 2020

The Planet Corona Archipelago

Here's an interesting fact that I picked up during my pre-Planet Corona travels. There are 1,200–6,000 Greek islands, with varying criteria as to what qualifies as an "island," and "only" about 227 of them are occupied.

I mention this, because of late I feel that Planet Corona is beginning to resemble an archipelago of islands with a lot of water in between where people are swimming, diving, and having a grand old time, calling out "Come on in, the waters fine!"

They are evidently oblivious to the ominous strains of the music from *Jaws* which is playing in the background! That is not to say that the waters are shark-infested. But you only *need one*! And those of us on the islands keep shouting "Watch out for that fin!" without anyone paying much attention.

So, I'm saying that many people on this planet (or at least my corner of it) are behaving as if we are totally post-corona (whatever that is going to look like, for that matter), when reality doesn't seem to sustain that overly optimistic point of view.

When you are outside, you see too many people who have given up wearing masks. Or else they have them on their persons either as a fashion statement (a necklace or bracelet) or as sports equipment (a chin guard), or else, unbeknownst to the rest of us, human physiology has changed and some people are beginning to breathe through their chins!

And you don't need the newspaper photos of crowded beaches and restaurants to know that social distancing is being measured by people who clearly have no concept of what 2 meters looks like. You can see evidence of that anywhere you look on the streets.

There was a time when I felt that Planet Corona was the "boat" of which it was said that we all were in the same one. Now, I wonder. Even people who ought to be "older and wiser" behave as though, "Well, now that it's over, we can all go back to our normal lives!"

Personally, I don't believe that anyone knows what "the new normal" is going to look like as the conditions and realities change every day. We also persist in a zigzag motion of "advancing" and then "retreating" as it dawns on at least some of us that we are perhaps acting in haste and often repenting those actions.

So, what do I (we?) do about the feeling that things are not quite right on Planet Corona? I think we have to own the fact that we don't need to compare our level of compliance and good sense with those of others.

One friend said that she felt a little silly being one of very few wearing masks at a family celebration. "And if 'everybody' jumps off the roof, are you going to, also?" asked the stereotypical (but wise) mother. Something to keep in mind.

Don't forget that the people who "know better" such as doctors, epidemiologists, and other informed and concerned people, are on our side. So, we are in good company. We also should be proactive in starting or continuing safe activities that give us pleasure. There are many. Sometimes I feel that I've never been quite this busy.

But, most of all, I think we need to "Let go and let God." We have *never* actually been in control and now there's simply more evidence of that fact. Being too involved in that which is not "your business" causes frustration and even pain. In addition, it occupies too much of your precious time. The following chart helps me to put into perspective what my real and worthwhile options are.

I cannot control (So, I can *let go* of these things):

1. Whether others follow the rules of social distancing
2. The actions of others
3. What may happen
4. Other people's motives
5. How others react
6. How long this will last

I can control (So, I will focus on these things):

1. My positive attitude
2. How I follow the rules
3. Turning off the news
4. Finding pleasant things to do at home
5. My own social distancing
6. Limiting my social media
7. My kindness and grace

My daughter shared a beautiful idea tonight that I want to pass on. In these very difficult and tumultuous times, we have no idea what the next day, or even the next hour, will bring. Our national and personal lives seem to be storm-tossed with new challenges arising with jarring frequency. She said that she wakes up each morning with no knowledge of what the day will bring, but with one prayer and resolve: "Let me be an "*Eved Hashem*"* today in whatever I do and with whatever comes my way."

I think we can do no better than that. Anywhere. At any time.

* Servant of God.

June 9, 2020

Planet Corona as Holland

Dedicated to the amazing and devoted parents of special-needs children whom I know and admire. And love.

One of the things that I probably like least about Planet Corona is that you can still get the Intergalactic edition of *The New York Times* here! Not my favorite publication. To say the least. As it is, I am trying to avoid almost all news. But the "News That's Fit to Print" (according to NY liberals, that is) is generally not on my reading list. However, today my husband left on our computer an article entitled "When 511 Epidemiologists Expect to Fly, Hug and Do 18 Other Everyday Activities Again."

It was very sobering. It suggested that it might be a rather long time before we can safely go to weddings, travel other than locally, have more than one or two guests over for a meal, or hug anyone let alone grandchildren! The article—along with other recent experiences, thoughts and events—caused me to wonder just how long our sojourn on Planet Corona is meant to be!

When I first arrived on the planet, after the initial shock, I found and wrote about some of the sometimes charming aspects of our new address. It was like arriving at any new destination. After the first period of to-be-expected disorientation, one begins to see interesting and even attractive aspects of the new surroundings.

Unless, of course, the new surroundings are irredeemably negative. Like if you've ended up in prison, the Sahara Desert, or in the middle of Times Square. (That one would work for me. You can choose your own bad places!) But the point is that most of the time, you don't expect to *remain indefinitely at* the new location.

We all know the old saw "It's a nice place to visit, but I wouldn't want to live there!" That saying has certainly been at the back of my mind all along. But now the thought has crept in that, although it appears that no one *really* knows how long we're going to be here, this could go on a lot longer than we expected.

I was reminded of a short essay that was given as an address by the parents of a special-needs child at a Yachad* gathering years ago. It is entitled "Welcome to Holland." At the time, I was under the impression that it was original to the parents. But it appears that Emily Perl Kingsley wrote "Welcome to Holland" in 1987. A parent of a child with Down syndrome, she wrote it to comfort other parents struggling to accept their own special needs situations.

I am appending the full text of the essay at the end of this letter but, in essence, she compares having a special-needs child to the experience of a person who had always looked forward to visiting Italy and planned this special trip to the last detail. However, when the plane lands, it turns out that she is not in Italy, but in Holland. At first, she is terribly disappointed, even horrified. But slowly, she recognizes that though Holland is not Italy, and even though she had always dreamt of seeing Italy, Holland also had its positive aspects, and even charms.

After reading the essay, you are forced to conclude that this could only legitimately have been written by someone who actually *has* such a child. Because it would be the height of chutzpa for someone not having this experience to have written such an upbeat essay.

I recently read an article written by Kristen Groseclose, also a parent of a special-needs child, which was somewhat critical of "Welcome to Holland." She felt that it trivialized the often painful aspects of having such a child. One of her difficulties with the essay is the impression that such an air-brushed description might give to other people about what it's like to have a developmentally challenged child.

> *Yes*, they may think, *Now I get it—a child with challenges is not something to grieve for, not really. It's more like an Oprah-approved "living your best life" kind of thing. Besides, you get windmills! And tulips! And don't forget about Rembrandt!*

Which is not to say, as Groseclose points out, that there aren't ever beautiful and special moments and experiences, but one cannot and must not overlook or minimize the huge challenges and great difficulties that are also part of the package. She offers an alternative view of her own experience:

> *'My barn having burned down, I can see the moon'*—Mizuta Masahide
> This haiku from a seventeenth-century Japanese poet and samurai speaks to the competing joys and sorrows of our situation. Destruction and hope in 10 short words.
>
> While the barn may symbolize the loss of our dreams, viewing the moon shows how our new reality does hold beauty and awe.

What does all the above have to do with being on Planet Corona? First of all, a caveat. I do not intend to *really* compare life on Planet Corona to life as a parent of a special-needs child! That would be totally out of proportion and trivializing of that experience. However, there are a few similarities. One is that having such a child is usually a long-term, even lifetime undertaking. It isn't something that happens and then you go on to the next thing.

The fact that our lives on Planet Corona may be heavily impacted for a significant time, for a much longer time than we originally imagined, is similarly very disquieting for many of us. *It wasn't what we expected!* It's one thing to call life here "the new normal." It's quite another to wonder what that "new normal" is going to look like and if there will ever again be "the old normal."

Another point that mirrors one that Groseclose makes, is that different people experience things differently. In her article, she says that there *are* people who are very much comforted by Kingsley's essay. And it is for their sakes that she adds the essay to the end of her article.

So, too, each of us on Planet Corona is experiencing this period in a unique way. What is a "charming" aspect to one person might be a "horror" to another. That is why the haiku that Groseclose finds helpful might also be helpful for us. We need to admit that the "barn has burnt down."

There have been many changes, and many of them are painful. But there is a "moon" out there, nonetheless. There are things we are seeing and experiencing that we haven't seen or experienced before. And, in adjusting to the new realities, we just might become greater selves.

WELCOME TO HOLLAND

By Emily Perl Kingsley

I am often asked to describe the experience of raising a child with a disability – to try to help people who have not shared that unique experience to understand it, to imagine how it would feel. It's like this.

When you're going to have a baby, it's like planning a fabulous vacation trip – to Italy. You buy a bunch of guide books and make your wonderful plans. The Coliseum. The Michelangelo David. The gondolas in Venice. You may learn some handy phrases in Italian. It's all very exciting.

After months of eager anticipation, the day finally arrives. You pack your bags and off you go. Several hours later, the plane lands. The stewardess comes in and says, "Welcome to Holland."

"Holland?!?" you say. "What do you mean Holland?? I signed up for Italy! I'm supposed to be in Italy. All my life I've dreamed of going to Italy."

But there's been a change in the flight plan. They've landed in Holland and there you must stay.

The important thing is that they haven't taken you to a horrible, disgusting, filthy place, full of pestilence, famine and disease. It's just a different place.

So, you must go out and buy new guide books. And you must learn a whole new language. And you will meet a whole new group of people you would never have met.

It's just a different place. It's slower-paced than Italy, less flashy than Italy. But after you've been there for a while and you catch your breath, you look around.... and you begin to notice that Holland has windmills.... and Holland has tulips. Holland even has Rembrandts.

But everyone you know is busy coming and going from Italy... and they're all bragging about what a wonderful time they had there. And for the rest of your life, you will say "Yes, that's where I was supposed to go. That's what I had planned."

And the pain of that will never, ever, ever, ever go away... because the loss of that dream is a very, very significant loss.

But... if you spend your life mourning the fact that you didn't get to Italy, you may never be free to enjoy the very special, the very lovely things... about Holland.

* Orthodox Union programming for youth with cognitive disabilities.

June 12, 2020

Harnessing the Elephant in the Room

There's an "elephant in the room" on Planet Corona which we frequently try to ignore or actually manage to occasionally forget during this period. While we try to derive lessons, suggest strategies, complain about rules of compliance or about the absence of compliance, the "elephant" looms over us casting its shadow everywhere. That "elephant" is called, not surprisingly, the coronavirus or Covid-19.

Yes, while many of us haven't been very heavily impacted by the actual illness, probably everyone knows of people who have had it and perhaps someone who, tragically, didn't survive it. However, if you don't live in the most heavily impacted areas in Israel or, even more so in the US, where the virus has hit hardest and claimed heavy casualties, chances are that you have been much more affected by the corollary effects of corona than by the disease itself. Which has led some people to be less than vigilant (sometimes, *much less*) and to act as if everything has gone back to normal when it hasn't.

It's time, perhaps, to remind people that this is potentially a very serious illness. Especially, but not exclusively, when it affects older people. You know, like people's parents or grandparents! (Something that I wish some "non-compliants" would think of more often!) You can read about how serious and even life-threatening the virus is in various places. And those are the survivors!

One such testimony that I would recommend is the video made by Dr. Yaakov Salomon, a psychotherapist from Brooklyn. He is a frequent contributor to the Aish Hatorah website and that's where this video can be found, *Rabbi Yaakov Salomon vs. Corona. The inside story of a survivor.*

His description of his experience with Covid-19 is very sobering and the five lessons that he derived from his illness and his recovery are instructive and inspirational. He speaks with great honesty and thought, and the video is a view into the world of the illness that the rest of us must pray never to experience directly.

At the end of the video there's a line that really imprinted itself onto my consciousness. He says that we should hope that, after all this is somehow behind us, we should be left "Not with what the pandemic did *to* us, but rather what the pandemic did *for* us!"

If there is anything that has occupied my thoughts and writing in the last three months, it's that thought. It's also what's been communicated by those I speak to and those I hear from. It's the message of the Ishay Ribo song "Keter Melucha." What are we supposed to take from all of this? What does Hashem want us to learn from all of this?

Not having had coronavirus, Baruch Hashem, I can't say what someone might take away from actually experiencing the illness. However, Rabbi Salomon, who had the full weight of the virus crash down upon him, *does* share his five lessons and I believe that they are "lessons from the trenches" and worth remembering and passing on.

1. During his illness, there were times when Dr. Salomon was totally helpless. Not only was he unable to eat a banana, he couldn't even *hold* a banana! He confesses to a very strong independent spirit and it had always been an important element in his makeup. He now puts forth a "Declaration of *Dependence*" saying that it is basic to all humanity that we are all dependent, on others and certainly on Hashem. And that our pride in our independence stems from that very source. Pride. Hubris. His understanding that we are always, in reality, dependent, is in fact liberating and humbling and essential for our understanding of how each individual and how society function.

2. Due to the extreme seriousness of his illness, Dr. Salomon, at critical points, was forced to face his own mortality. In a very real and powerful way. He very openly speaks of his discovery that he, in his innermost self, proved to be more fearful of dying than he would have imagined before his illness. His own "take" is that we need to "face our fears" before they overtake and overpower us. But we can also face up to our own mortality and recognize more fully that which we already know, which is that "no one leaves this earth alive" and therefore we should commit to living our lives to the fullest, most deeply, nurturing our relationships, our spiritual selves, and our connection to Hashem.

3. He discovered that, in terms of his *bitachon*, his trust, in Hashem, he was not quite where he had believed himself to be. His message is that, as you cannot really trust "anyone" whom you do not "know," you must bring Hashem more into your conscious existence in order to empower your bitachon. He adds that this quality is not a "have it" or "don't have it" proposition. Measures of bitachon are on a shifting continuum which must be constantly monitored and nourished.

4. One of his very unexpected discoveries was that, even at the point when the crisis had passed and he was recovering, he found himself to be worried, nervous, and fragile. This surprised him. He began to realize that these feelings were due to the negative stimulation he was receiving from the news, social media,

and other sources of "information." We are under the mistaken impression, he adds, that "information = power and control." He vehemently disagrees, saying that this negative input actually saps our strength. He sees it as an unhealthy addiction and found that his mood and health improved greatly when he limited his media intake to what was practical and necessary.

5. Being a psychotherapist, it is not at all surprising that his fifth lesson is about the power of speech and of communicating. He says that he *had* and *has* an overwhelming need to talk about and share his experience. Clearly, that's why he made the video. He describes it as "letting the pus out." One of the "pluses" of our sojourn on Planet Corona is that, deprived of other occupations and opportunities for human interaction, many of us are talking, writing, and communicating more, even if in many cases it is virtually. We are sharing our experiences, our reactions, our trials and challenges, and our coping mechanisms. We are also sharing inspirational messages and ideas. This is all very positive and necessary.

I really hope and pray that, despite the fact that no one wanted this pandemic, and although this has been and continues to be a most serious health crisis with life-threatening potential, we can learn lessons, improve ourselves, and help make a better post-pandemic world than the pre-pandemic world that we once knew.

June 18, 2020

A Visit to the Kotel

Yesterday morning I went to the Kotel* for the first time in many months. Today, I went again. Yes, you can get there from Planet Corona. But don't ask me how. It was a very special experience. In the past, I have been used to the summer crowds in the Old City, tourists from around the world, usually Christian but not exclusively, standing in long lines to visit the Temple Mount or going to "The Wall" to pray in various languages and, in some cases, to a variety of deities. There was great energy there and I always felt vitalized by the sparkling and positive atmosphere, that facet of Yerushalayim as "the Center of the World" that I often found exhilarating.

How different on Planet Corona. A beautiful summer day and the Kotel plaza with its many white-curtained cubicles each surrounding a handful of praying women. Disc-shaped stickers on the ground with the outlines of a pair of feet to remind and help people to maintain social distance. A sprinkling of women and girls at the Kotel itself, keeping a safe distance between themselves or being reminded to do so by the special team of "Corona guards" recently employed to help keep the Kotel plaza a safe venue.

As I entered the Old City walls and approached the plaza, I saw Sara, an olah** I know who works at one of the information booths. I'm a little in awe of Sara, who writes thoughtful poetry in Hebrew which is not her native tongue. She always shares with me her newest poem or some interesting Jewish thought or nugget from the parsha. Knowing that I am a teacher, she asks for my ideas on the subject.

Yesterday, she wanted to share an idea from the previous week's parsha, Shelach. The spies, she points out, didn't actually add 40 years to the People of Israel's wanderings. They added, in fact, 38 years as they were already in the second year from the Exodus when the incident occurred.

Sara suggested an interesting parallel that I had never heard before, namely that the Land of Israel must have endured great pain at being forced to wait an extra 38 years for her people to arrive and settle. She then compared that to the 38 years that Sarah Imenu had to wait for her husband Abraham to pass from the world and to come to be with her in Ma'arat Hamachpela.*** I added that there is a beautiful midrash that describes Abraham and Sarah lying in an eternal embrace within the burial cave. I thanked her for her insight and went on to daven at the Kotel.

At the Kotel, I found a place where I could be with the stones and with Hashem and safely distant from others. Partly because

I hadn't been there in so long, I found that my tefillot were more inspired and inspiring than usual. And I was so grateful to have this wonderful place to go to, within a short drive of my home. What a blessing.

All of this made me think of something I heard from Rabbi Manis Friedman a day or two ago on a video in which he says that this pandemic has helped us to strip away "the stuff," the inessentials, from our relationships, experiences, and activities and get down to the core, the real essence of all those elements of our existence.

When you strip your friendships of the "let's do lunch," shopping trips, and entertainment gatherings, you're left with just you and your friend and your need for each other's empathy and companionship. When you can no longer go to the gym with the fancy equipment, Pilates classes, and saunas, you discover that healthful exercise can also be obtained by a brisk walk or a video on your laptop. And you don't need to search for a parking space. And you can use your membership fee for something more important.

When the Kotel is not a huge tourist attraction, a magnet for visitors and worshippers, then it's "just" those ancient stones with "human hearts" and the dream of the to-be-rebuilt Beit Hamikdash, and you with your prayers and hopes and desire to come closer to Hashem. Also, Sara with her inspirational poetry and interesting ideas.

And Yerushalayim, when it is not the busy, bustling, summer vacation magnet, is just what it has always been at its core. The beautiful city containing 90 percent of all earthly charm. The ancient capital of the Jewish people, beloved for millennia both by those who dwell there and those who yearn to be there.

And to me, it's home.

* The Western Wall.
** Immigrant to Israel. Fem.
*** Cave of the Patriarchs.

June 24, 2020

Pay Attention!

When did we first begin our voyage to Planet Corona? It appears that we were on our way for quite a while before we realized that we had actually arrived some time earlier. I only noticed that I was on a new planet about midway between Purim and Pesach. However, the first case of Covid-19 was reported on November 17, 2019. Then, we were on the way. Only we didn't realize it at that time!

Interestingly, that date corresponds to the 19th of Marcheshvan and *that* suggests a rather interesting correlation between our Coronavirus experience and the process of repentance and steadily increasing deprivations connected to the withholding of rain as it is described in Masechet Taanit.

In Israel, we begin praying for rain on the 7th of Marcheshvan. But on the 17th of Marcheshvan the procedures delineated in M. Taanit begin to be set in motion. This year, that date corresponded to November 15, just two days before the first coronavirus case was reported. The Mishna then describes the increasingly stringent measures to be taken in the process of repentance which it is hoped will bring about the release of the rains.

First, the bathhouses were to be closed (swimming pools, *mikvaot**). Then shops were to be shuttered (malls, clothing stores, restaurants, etc.), but they did allow food stores to be open in order to honor Shabbat. If the rains still hadn't come, they began to restrict all types of business, farm work, and building. They then proceeded to restrict "betrothals and weddings" (presumably, wedding halls took a hit!).

And then the ultimate restriction. People would no longer greet their fellow (social distancing, anyone!?!). "As if they were people undesirable to God!" Strong language, indeed! These practices and deprivations continue until after Nissan if the rains do not arrive by then.

At this point, the Mishna goes on to prescribe the different acts and prayers of supplication and repentance that should be undertaken. One is the wearing of sackcloth and ashes. The Mishna cites as its source the Book of Jonah which describes the repentance of the people of Nineveh which saved them from destruction. However, it's pointed out that it is written in Jonah that "God saw their *deeds...*" Not their *ashes*, but their *deeds*.

I was introduced to the above analysis by my son Akiva who had been studying M. Taanit with his chavruta and was struck powerfully by the analogies. The question obviously is, what's the significance of all this for *us*? After all, we have not suffered a drought this year. Quite the opposite. We were blessed with abundant rain.

I am presently in the Galilee with a beautiful view of the Kineret (the Sea of Galilee), fuller than it's been in a very long time. However, along with the bountiful rain this year from Cheshvan through Nissan, we had a "bountiful".... *coronavirus epidemic.*

All of the various stages described in M. Taanit which we are instructed to *initiate* in order to bring us to repentance and moral improvement, were *imposed* upon us by the Covid-19 epidemic. The withholding of rain is meant as a "wake-up call" to the Jewish people to look deeply into their actions and to repair that which is impaired.

So, too, this period of crisis which we are living through, should have been and still should be a similar call to reflection and repair. Lack of rain, *geshem*, strikes powerfully at the entire physical and material framework of our lives, our *gashmiyut*. So has this period of corona crisis. The material foundations of our individual and even global lives have been earth-shakingly undermined.

At the beginning of our consciousness of the powerful nature of this epidemic and its consequences, many felt that Hashem was trying to get our attention. By stripping away much of the distractions of our habituated lives, perhaps He would proceed by telling us what He was calling upon us to do, to understand, to restructure.

Ishay Ribo reflected that in his song "Keter Melucha," with its refrain, "What is it that You want from us?" We thought that after Hashem demanded that we, "*Pay attention*!!" he would subsequently tell the World how it should change. How *we* should change.

And we awaited the Call from On High. But, if and when "It" came, it wasn't clear and unambiguous. Even for those whose inclination was to actually *try* and hear the Call (and that inclination wasn't universal, by any means), what they "heard" was what they wanted or expected to hear. So, they put forth varied theories as to what, exactly, Hashem "wants from us" (or more often, "from *them*"). But there was certainly no unifying consensus as to what "It" was.

However, perhaps the call to "*Pay Attention!*" *is* the message. Perhaps we are being told to live deliberately and consciously, to revisit our habituations, to be in the present, to practice our God-given gift of "free choice," Maybe we have been awakened to recognize Hashem as a constant Presence and Active Participant (at the very least!) in our world and in our lives.

The Kotsker Rebbe's famous answer to the question of "Where is Hashem?" is "Wherever you let Him in!" That suggests that Hashem is "real and present" for us, to the extent that we make ourselves conscious of and sensitive to His Presence and Influence.

In his book, *Seeing God*, Rabbi David Aaron relates an experience of a friend who attended a sold-out concert near Tel Aviv. As he was making his way to his seat, he saw a family with children climbing over the fence to get in, after first looking to the right and to the left to make sure no one was watching. The friend went over to them and asked, "What are you doing?" The father replied, "It's none of your business!" The friend responded, "I noticed that you looked to the right and to the left. But you didn't look *up*!"

If we actually would heed the message of "Pay Attention!" to truly recognize Hashem's *constant and uninterrupted* presence and involvement in our lives, we would probably behave differently. We might think about all the "highlighted" areas that were affected during our crisis. Business was affected. Have we dealt fairly and honestly in all our business dealings and in the workplace? Celebrations were curtailed. Does Hashem really want us to impoverish ourselves in order to celebrate important occasions?

Batei Knesset** were closed. What is the quality of our tefillot and our attendance at a minyan? Do we come to daven or to socialize? Our social and family interactions were impeded. How do we treat others? How do we speak to them and about them? And how might all that be improved upon if we *really* "paid attention?" If we truly *knew* that Hashem observes, judges, and prescribes? If we honestly *believed* that Hashem is always in our lives?

And acted upon that belief!

* Ritual baths.
** Synagogues.

June 25, 2020

STUFF: Part 1

We are presently coming to the end of a short vacation in the northern region of the Holyland on Planet Corona. We are in a cabin (with all the amenities) in an idyllic setting which has afforded me much time to think about our present situation, which appears to be worsening rather than improving. So, I've been thinking about "stuff," All sorts of "stuff."

When you pack for a vacation, of course you think of all the things you will need. Or, if you're like me, the things that there's even a *remote* chance you *might* need! You pack it all and you're on your way. If you've packed carefully and well, you will find that you are comfortably covered, with a little to spare, for the length of your stay and the type of vacation.

For instance, since we were planning to stay in a cabin, and because we were only going to eat out occasionally because of the epidemic, I brought some kitchen items to supplement what was already in the cabin, in order to warm up food and do some light cooking. Since we are leaving for home in about an hour, I can see that I planned and packed pretty well this time.

But what if it turned out that, for some reason, we discovered we were going to have to be here for a considerably longer period? And what if I couldn't supplement what I'd brought with me? Well, I would have to make do with what I have.

I could handwash the clothing, and prepare very simple meals as long as it would be possible to at least purchase staples. I might surprise myself and discover that the amount of "stuff" that I brought for less than a week might, in a pinch, serve for a significantly longer time.

Since one of the "gifts" of this vacation was having more time than usual to do some pondering, I've been thinking of the "stuff" in my life of all kinds, material, emotional, and spiritual. How much of it do I actually *need* and of how much could I rid myself to the actual betterment of my life?

In the Book of Jonah, we are told of Jonah's experience on the storm-tossed sea when the mariners are jettisoning items off the ship until Yonah proves to them that *he, himself,* must be thrown overboard! On a sailing vessel, or even on The Ship of Life, traveling with too heavy a load, with too much "stuff" (of all kinds!) makes travel, at the very least, very cumbersome, and even, potentially, life-threatening.

I recently heard a pre-corona travel story about my daughter-in-law's cousin, who was on a domestic flight in the US with his wife and daughter on their way to a wedding. Shortly before takeoff there was an announcement that the flight was "overweight," and they were looking for volunteers who would agree to disembark and take a later flight. Every volunteer would receive as compensation a $3,000 (!) credit for future travel.

The cousin and family quickly volunteered after ascertaining that a later flight would still get them to their destination in time for the wedding. Not only did the family make a huge profit but the cousin confided that he also wasn't sure he wanted to actually *be* on a flight where the weight of three people (his wife and daughter are pretty thin!) plus luggage represented the difference between a plane flying safely and not being able to get off the ground!

I know that I have too many belongings. I think many of us can relate to that. We even pay other people to help us decide what to get rid of. I remember when I spent my junior year in Israel and how surprised my Israeli dorm mates were when we Americans complained that the closets were so small, while they thought they were more than sufficiently roomy! And it has only gone downhill from there.

My grandchildren have many more toys and playthings than my children did, and my children had much more than I had growing up. More toys, more clothes, more sports equipment. More "stuff." So we need "walk-in" closets, larger houses, and more time to maintain, clean, and organize all these belongings. Not to speak of the hard-earned money that is spent to purchase the "stuff!"

And the thing is, we *know* that we don't really "need" so much. But we are too easily influenced by the media, by ads, by glossy magazines whose raison d'être appears to be to cause us to feel somehow inadequate if we don't have nicely furnished homes, a large and varied wardrobe, gourmet food that we can either purchase or prepare (and don't forget the "beautiful presentation!").

If we're honest with ourselves, we can each contribute an almost endless list of unnecessary "stuff" in our own lives. We're told by our Chachamim* that we'll never be satisfied that we have even "half enough" material belongings if that's what's important to us. Many of us have heard the story of "Reichman's Socks" (if not, it's at the end of this letter), but has the message truly penetrated?

A few years ago, when I thought along the lines of the preceding paragraphs, I decided to go on a "purchasing fast." I determined not to buy anything at all for myself, not even a hairpin, for six months. It was wonderful! I felt so light. It left me time for other, more important occupations.

It's time for me to think once again about what my real needs are. Perhaps my sojourn on Planet Corona will help me put my material "stuff" into a true and meaningful perspective that will allow me to jettison what is weighing me down and result in my traveling lighter and better.

This story may be apocryphal. Or not. Either way, it's a very good story.

MR. REICHMAN'S SOCKS

Old, Orthodox, and very rich Mr. Reichman was clearly on his deathbed. When he seemed to be nearing the end, he called in his family and said, "Soon, I will no longer be with you and I have a request to make that I ask you most urgently to fulfill." After the family members tearfully assured him that he would live until 120, they agreed to fulfill his last request.

Mr. Reichman continued, "The socks that I am wearing are my favorite item of clothing. I wish to be buried in them." Bewildered, but having already committed themselves, the family agreed to follow his instructions. He then gave his children a sealed envelope which he said contained a message for them to be read before they got up from sitting shiva.

After he passed on, his family relayed his last request to the Chevra Kadisha (burial society), but were told that his request was an impossibility as the *tachrichim* (burial shrouds) in which Jews are traditionally laid to rest are the same for all, nothing can be added or subtracted or changed in any way. Therefore, they did not permit using the deceased's socks.

The family members were stricken. They had promised. The children went to their Orthodox family rabbi and begged him to intervene for them. However, he reiterated the traditional stand presented by the Chevra Kadisha and said that, unfortunately, there was nothing he could do.

So, Mr. Reichman was buried in the traditional linen shrouds and without his "favorite socks," and his heirs tried to come to terms with the fact that they were unable to fulfill his last request.

When shiva was over and the family was about to get up and disperse, the oldest son remembered the sealed envelope. He took it out of his pocket, opened it and read the following, "By now you know that you can't take *anything* with you. Not even a pair of socks!"

* The Sages.

Chapter Five

July 2020

STUFF: Part 2

It's pretty clear that we are still on Planet Corona, despite the fact that there are those who speak and write of "the post-corona" period. The numbers of cases and the spread of the virus show this to be unassailably true. However, I am beginning to wonder what the nature of this planet is.

At the start, and for some time after, I was convinced that Planet Corona was a novel place of *habitation* for some indeterminate amount of time. It appears to me today, that it might in fact be more of a *journey* with ever-changing vistas than an address.

This reminds me of the scientific breakthrough of the early 20th century, which proved, through quantum mechanics, that light was *both* a particle *and* a wave. Moreover, it could be *both* simultaneously! So, is Planet Corona an address or a journey? Or both?

The reason for my doubts is that, whereas at the beginning of our sojourn here all the inhabitants of this planet seemed to be facing the same challenges with similar battle plans and approaches, today we all seem to be at different stages of our journey through this unique and almost unfathomable experience.

Unfortunately, this has also resulted in much confusion, radically different adherence to "the rules," and even conflicting ideas of what "normal" is or should be. At times, many of us feel that we are in a turbulent and chaotic place. And current events, particularly in the US, only add to these feelings and apprehensions.

Not only that, but I begin to understand, at least on some level, why people *are* in fact in different places from me and my cohort. It's due to differences in age, family situation, financial situation, even politics.

Today, I received a humorous cartoon of a doctor and patient. The patient asks, "Doctor, how long do you think this Covid-19 epidemic will last?" The doctor replies, "I don't know. I'm not much into politics." I'm not saying that I necessarily agree with the actions being taken by others. But I do at least understand a little of the motivation. Besides, there isn't much that I can do to influence the actions of others. I can only work on myself. Which is probably all that anyone can *ever* do.

This is all by way of an introduction to STUFF: Part 2. In Part 1, I focused on the *material* "stuff" that we might wish to jettison in order to "travel more lightly" now and in the future. Hopefully, we have discovered while on Planet Corona that we probably have more of almost everything material than we need and that "more" is sometimes "less" when we realize how this "muchness" impacts on our lives.

But some of the "stuff" we carry with us, and which is often a burden to us, is not material. It is emotional, ideological, and behavioral. It includes dearly held misconceptions and preconceptions. Because it's "ours," this "stuff" is very difficult to dump. But we have had time and still have opportunities to review and re-evaluate and separate it all into two piles—"Keep" and "Discard."

If we have heretofore been living rather frenetic lives (mea culpa!), we have hopefully discovered by now that slowing down *voluntarily* can be refreshing, relaxing, soothing, and healing. Reducing our pace of living offers more opportunities for reflection, study, or simple "down-time," permitting our minds to wander for a bit and perhaps take us to unexpected places. So, *keep* the slower-pace and *discard* the frenzy,

Along with a frenetic lifestyle generally goes micro-managing. Even though many of us ostensibly believe that Hashem is always in charge and *Ein od Milvado*, sometimes we act in ways that belie that belief. We think, "If I don't do it, it won't get done. And, anyway, I'm the one who can really do this best."

If we've learned anything from our stay on Planet Corona, it's that we are *not in charge*! Not in the least. For the most part, it doesn't even seem as if any human is! Everyone appears to be at a loss. So, "Let Go and Let God!" Not only does it relieve anxiety, stress, and burdensome responsibility, it also reflects a better understanding of *reality*, on Corona or elsewhere. *Keep* your *bitachon* and *discard* your hubris.

I have made several discoveries myself. I have found that a Shabbat or Chag meal with "just" my husband is not a situation that must be avoided. These meals are surprisingly relaxed, spiritually uplifting, and totally in keeping with the specialness of the day.

I think I will *discard* my former idea that a Shabbat table must be crowded to be properly "*shabbosdik*" (Shabbat appropriate) and *keep* smaller and more intimate meals, where you really get to know the person or people you are with. To be honest, when it is again possible to have a larger number of guests, I probably will on occasion. But not as a necessity.

I will certainly want to *keep* all my wonderful family and friends. They are the greatest treasures of my life! But I can *discard* much of the "eating out" which had become an almost inextricable part of my social interactions. It is expensive and frequently unnecessary. Restaurant eating should be an occasional treat rather than a social must.

We have met with people in our garden (with appropriate social distancing, of course). At this point, the most that some of them will allow us to offer is self-served water. But the conversation and conviviality are not at all diminished. Perhaps the opposite is true as there are fewer distractions.

My stay on Planet Corona has certainly enhanced my empathy for my fellow humans. But these days that empathy is feeling somewhat strained. I am unhappy with those who refuse to comply with the rules, often out of laziness, disinterest, and even selfishness. Or so it would seem.

But I need to remind myself that other people's motivations are generally unknown to me, and therefore I can't possibly place myself as a judge of their actions. I am obligated to "judge favorably" or preferably, not to judge *at all*. So, I should *keep* my warm feelings of kinship with others and *discard* judgementalism. We can only work on ourselves and pray that others do likewise.

Now that I have begun my "Keep" and "Discard" piles, I think I'll continue to work on organizing my "stuff" of all kinds and watch the piles get higher. At least, it's a worthwhile occupation to keep one busy during our "Corona Days."

July 7, 2020

Like a Bridge Over Running Water

It was running water that began to effect a turn-around in my spirits. Or rather, the sound of running water in my kitchen while I was davening this morning. But, to backtrack a bit.

Yesterday, probably for the first time since arriving on Planet Corona, I really wanted to go to bed at night and wake up somewhere else. Almost anywhere else. (Although, when I shared this idea with my sister, she commented, "You don't really mean that. There are much worse places and situations!" Of course, she's right.) Still, I had found the worsening situation to be very worrisome.

Although my personal situation is probably an enviable one—i.e., no children home all day, no financial worries, good health, good company, etc.—I was affected by the difficulties of those around me, particularly family. It was just "too much."

Yesterday afternoon, we were visited by a couple we know who sat, with appropriate distancing, in our garden. I expressed some of my personal worries and distress over the current situation after my friends had shared some of the disappointments they've been experiencing. For one thing, some of their grown children in the US had planned to visit them here in Israel. But, of course, that was not going to happen.

Nonetheless, these friends were quite upbeat and optimistic. They emphasized some of the more positive consequences and even benefits of this period in time. Then the wife turned to me and said, "There *are* some good things coming out of this crisis. You know, like you write about in your Letters." Well, that certainly put me in my place! Doctor, heal thyself.

Still, I was finding it difficult to completely shake off my low spirits. In the morning, the first two things that happened in rapid succession were that I discovered that we had no running water and that, very tragically, a married son of friends of ours had passed away yesterday. I was terribly upset and shaken by the news. What was going on here on this Planet!?!

My husband called the water company and found that there was a broken main that was being repaired. The lack of water was "just" an annoyance. But it *was* that.

I dressed and began to daven. Midway through my tefillot, my husband went into the kitchen and tried the water taps and the water was flowing! I heard the music of the running water and, rather surprisingly, it began to lift my spirits. I do not mean to minimize the tragedy that we had become aware of. Our friends' terrible loss lay heavy.

But I began to think of all the things, simple and not so simple, that we take for granted until they are removed temporarily or, sometimes, even permanently. "Simple" but necessary things like running water inside your home, plentiful and at the required temperature being only one example.

I remembered the stories that my father would tell of his family's poverty, when the first thing he had to do in winter upon awakening was to break the ice in the pail in order to wash his hands! It was never more than an interesting story to me. Today, I remembered those tales.

Any certainty that we ever thought we had of what the new day would bring is gone. The situation and the rules change almost daily. There is great distress surrounding this uncertainty. It leaves you feeling very unbalanced. In truth, that's the way it always is and has been. But we've never been so aware of this.

And at the epicenter of all this confusion and discomfort is the question of emuna and bitachon. As my sister mused out loud today, "Where *is* my emuna?" I seconded the question. She continued to point out that there has never been a time in our memory when it was so obvious that Hashem was the *only* One in charge. All illusions we had entertained as to our part in the running of the world have been stripped away.

My sister said that she had been very inspired by the words of her friend's 80-year-old mother. When asked if she was afraid at this time, she answered, "I am only afraid of the things that man can do. Not of the things that Hashem does." *That* is enviable emuna and bitachon.

I recently read an inspirational message on emuna, connected to the *Parah Adumah* (the Red Heifer) and its juxtaposition to the death of Miriam. We've been taught that the Parah Adumah is the ultimate *chok*, a law that defies all logic and human understanding. It is introduced as "This is the *Torah* of the Parah Adumah." This is to emphasize that our adherence to *chukim* (pl. of chok) best illustrates our emuna in Hashem, which is the essence of all Torah.

Then what is the relationship of the Red Heifer to the death of Miriam? The commentaries struggle with the question of why Miriam died in the desert. After all, she did not hit the rock, as her brothers did. Also, the Midrash stipulates that the women of Am Yisrael were not involved in the sin of the spies and were therefore not sentenced to die in the desert.

Different commentaries offer various answers, but it appears that the question remains just that, a mystery. For in fact, the death of tzaddikim, righteous ones, is one of the deepest and most troubling of questions.

"Why bad things happen to good people" is a mystery that even Moses could not fathom, and which constitutes an area of philosophy called theodicy. The death of Miriam is also in the same category as a chok, a troubling and unanswerable riddle that challenges, in the deepest way possible, our emuna in Hashem. Our unquestioning faith and acceptance is the strongest proof of our true belief in and dependence on Hashem.

Our reality has changed. Even the "new normal" varies from day to day. We sometimes feel that the terra firma beneath our feet isn't firm at all. To live with this situation is to take each day as it comes. To emphasize all the good and inspirational words and experiences that come our way. To nurture an "attitude of gratitude" and even write down a list of things for which we are grateful at the end of each day.

It's a constant challenge, an uphill battle which is not letting up. So, we have to hold on and not let up ourselves.

If the foundation doesn't seem firm, then *we* must be firm in our positive outlook, in finding contentment in our relationships and in our situations.

Look what the sound of running water can accomplish.

July 16, 2020

The Ubiquitous Elbow

There is a Letter from Planet Corona almost completed on my computer. I intend to finish it shortly and send it off. However, I decided today to take a short respite from all the seriousness of our present sojourn on this planet and share a somewhat lighter aspect of our situation.

One of my readers told me that she had particularly enjoyed my letter that focused on "the Hand." However, as I sneezed into the crook of my arm the other day (the crook being the *inside* of my elbow) I began to think about the outsized importance of "the Elbow" on the Plant Corona.

The elbow is not a part of the body that we think about very much. People have knee replacements, but not elbow replacements. You pay attention to your elbow when you hit your "funny bone" (which isn't particularly funny!) and, if you are very scrupulous in the laws of *tzniyut*,* then you take care to see that it is covered by your sleeve.

It appears that the only health issue that former US secretary of state Hillary Clinton ever had was breaking her elbow and if you look up quotes on the subject of the elbow it's hard to find anything even mildly inspirational. There *are* phrases with the word "elbow" in them. Some give employment to physical therapists such as "tennis elbow," "golfers elbow," and "miners elbow." (Ah, the perils of upper-class sports and lower-class labor!) Others suggest that our elbows help preserve our social distancing such as "elbow room" and "elbowing one's way."

Another phrase is appropriate for difficult physical exertion, that being "elbow grease". (Why would anyone want or need to apply grease to their elbow, anyway?). If your clothing is kind of old and worn, then you appear to be "out at the elbow." (Does anyone say that, anymore?) You wouldn't care to have an obnoxious person always "at your elbow," although small children often seem to be.

But you get to Planet Corona and all of a sudden we seem to be "all elbows." We sneeze and cough into our elbow so as not to get very bad stuff onto our hands and elsewhere. I've discovered that if you don't have too plump an elbow ("dimpled" if you are an infant or a Victorian heroine), it's very useful for pressing buttons in elevators, turning on certain water faucets, ringing doorbells, etc.

Elbows have even replaced hands as being useful for shaking and saying, "Nice to meet you." Although, since that is next to impossible to do with social distancing, unless you are a giant, it isn't as useful a gesture as it once might have been. And we've already mentioned the "elbow room" (of at least 2 meters!) that is necessary to maintain in order not to spread the virus.

There is also an "elbow story" that I recall hearing years ago that I thought might be appropriate for this planet and for those living here. I searched for it and found the following version:

I am told the story of a Rabbi. His name was Rabbi Chaim who traveled from town to town delivering religious sermons that stressed the importance of respect for one's fellow man. He often began his talks with the following story:

"I once ascended to the firmaments. I first went to see Gehinnom and the sight was horrifying. Row after row of tables were laden with platters of sumptuous food, yet the people seated around the tables were pale and emaciated, moaning with hunger. As I came closer, I understood their predicament. Every person held a full spoon. But their arms were splinted with wooden slats, so they could not bend either elbow to bring the food to their mouths. It broke my heart to hear the tortured groans of these poor people as they held their food so near, but could not consume it.

"Next, I went to visit Gan Eden. I was surprised to see the same setting I had witnessed in Gehinnom—row after row of long tables laden with food. However, in contrast, the people here in Gan Eden were sitting contentedly talking with each other, obviously sated from their sumptuous meal. As I came closer, I was amazed to discover that here, too, each person had his arms splinted on wooden slats that prevented him from bending his elbows. How, then, did they manage to eat?

"As I watched, a man picked up his spoon and dug it into the dish before him. Then he stretched across the table and fed the person across from him! The recipient of this kindness thanked him and returned the favor by leaning forward to feed his benefactor. I suddenly understood. Gan Eden and Gehinnom offer the same circumstances and conditions. The critical difference lies in the way the people treat each other."

This story reminds me of a recent incident. I went to our local *makolet* where I have been doing most of my shopping during the pandemic. People there generally wear masks and keep a reasonable distance away from each other. However, as I was about to enter I saw a young man without a mask waiting to pay for his items. In order to enter the store, I would have been forced to pass near him, so I waited at the entrance. He saw me there and indicated that there was room to pass by him. I said, "Maybe. But, you are not wearing a mask, so I'll wait."

When he finished paying and exited, he said rather sheepishly in Hebrew, "I'm sorry. You're right." I smiled and said, "I'm sure you have a *savta*. Well, I'm also someone's savta." He once again apologized and left. While I was still shopping he returned, having forgotten an item. This time he was wearing a mask.

Perhaps we are, indeed, all elbowed out. We can't seem to be able to help ourselves much or even protect ourselves. Everything is in confusion. But we can still try to help the *other person*, wear a mask to protect *them*, offer to help those who need assistance or a kind word, or even aid someone in finding a job. It's a choice we have, to make Planet Corona either a Gan Eden or a Gehinnom. It's up to us.

* Modesty.

July 17, 2020

What I Know (Not Much!) and What I (Have To) Believe

I have to be honest. I have never studied Biblical Criticism, particularly the "documentary hypothesis" and, frankly, I have no intention of doing so. Therefore, I hope I will not be guilty of seriously over-simplifying and misunderstanding. However, concerning what I *do* know about it, my strongest objection is that it removes or, at least, irons over the complexities, rigorous textual analysis, and deep messages of the most sacred of our texts, the Torah.

Leaving Divine authorship aside for a moment, the idea that the apparent contradictions, different names of Hashem, and the varied "voices" of the Bible text can all be explained by a hypothesis that the Torah is a cobbled-together work written at different times by different authors essentially obliterates almost all of the traditional Torah scholarship over the millennia.

It effaces the nuanced understanding of the infinite complexity of Hashem's Self-Revelation and participation in our history and lives. The "omnisignificance" of the text, which is infinitely enriching in positing that every word, letter, and apposition in the Torah is meaningful, consequently disappears. The "Seventy Faces" of the Torah lose all 70 levels of vitality.

In the study of the Talmud, "resolving" contradictions by saying that there are variant manuscripts, and that opposing opinions and conflicts arise from being based on different texts and scribal error, would obviate all the attempts by the Rabbis to resolve the conflicts by highlighting the truths of either side and the commonalities of both opinions.

I am not saying that there are *no* examples of varying texts and scribal error. There are many. The Talmud itself, on many occasions, will show that part of the quoted text is missing and will give the "corrected" version. Great rabbis and scholars have listed varying texts and these emendations have largely been adopted by traditional Talmudic scholars throughout the ages.

But where these variant texts have not been traditionally adopted, each additional attempt by academic analysis at "explaining away" contradictions in this way erases some deeper understanding and enriching subtlety that is at the source of Talmud study.

This rather lengthy introduction leads me to one of the main reasons that I do not choose (after all, it *is* a choice!) to see our current crisis as something terrible that "just happened," I choose to search or to be on the lookout for the meaning and lessons that are visible or can be derived from all the elements of our "new normal" lives. Because if this unprecedented and world-shaking episode in our history doesn't, essentially, *force* us to derive every bit of meaning that we can, then what a waste!

In his book *When Bad Things Happen to Good People*, Rabbi Harold Kushner, whose own son died tragically at the age of 14, develops the idea that there are tragedies in life that do not have religious meaning, because Hashem either chooses not to do, or "cannot" do, anything to intervene. There are, in fact, some things that do "just happen."

One purpose of this approach is to reduce the guilt and ensuing pain resulting from the idea that there is some sort of "punishment" involved in such events which would suggest that either the victim or the survivors were somehow guilty and deserved punishment. While this purpose might appear laudatory, it also results in stripping the event of meaning.

Years ago, when a friend of mine was facing great personal challenges and pain, I thought to present her with Kushner's book. Fortunately, I read it first. I strongly believed that, despite the pain involved, my friend would prefer trusting that her experiences had deep personal and religious significance rather than to somehow be placated. I did not give her the book and years later, when I related what had happened, she told me that my instincts had been correct.

Viktor Frankl, Holocaust survivor and father of logotherapy, refers to man's "will to meaning" and writes that "the last of human freedoms" is the ability to "choose one's attitude in a given set of circumstances." If Frankl, who describes the horrific experiences he underwent during the Holocaust, can use his experiences and survival to promote this powerful form of therapy, then his ideas are certainly applicable in our current situation.

On a more personal level, my father, a"h, himself a Holocaust survivor, emerged afterwards with an undiminished, and perhaps, even greater emuna and connection to Hashem. And he was not alone. Therefore, shouldn't we—who are presently in the midst of a crisis that, with all its difficulties, still does not come even close to the horrors and devastation of the Shoah—be diligently searching for religious meaning in this experience?

For me, the deepest meaning in this pandemic is feeling Hashem's presence in everything that is occurring. Therefore, here are some of the uncertainties, confusions, and "unknowables" on Planet Corona. But, alongside them, are some of the foundational beliefs and religious pillars that perhaps have been strengthened for us due to this crisis. And are a reminder of our own responsibilities.

1. People have been sick, some of them very sick indeed. Others have been taken from the world. We can't understand why they have been the ones designated for suffering and even death.

   However, I (have to) believe that while Hashem is the One Who inflicts sickness and pain, He is also the "*Rofeh Cholim*," the One Who cures the ill. Our days are calculated exactly, and we leave the world when and how we were meant to. That does not mean we should be fatalistic and careless. Follow the rules, wear a mask, keep social distance. But trust in Hashem.

2. The financial health of many, many people has been severely undermined. People have lost their means of making a living and are facing financial hardship.

   However, I (have to) believe that last Rosh Hashana the finances of each individual had already been determined, except for the money spent on Shabbat and Holidays and in the performance of mitzvot. We all have the financial resources we were meant to have. This does not, of course, absolve those of us who have the means from helping those who are presently in need.

3. So much of our social and religious lives have been severely curtailed or even "put on hold." It's affecting our family relationships, our friendships, and our celebrations. For the first time in our lives, we have no idea if there will be communal prayer on Rosh Hashana and Yom Kippur (the *only* days, for some Jews, when they connect to their religious heritage).

However, I (have to) believe that Hashem cherishes our family life, the interactive fabric of Jewish peoplehood, our prayers and Shabbatot and holidays. He desires them, but sees that very often they are not what they ought to be. So, He is affording us a chance to revisit these areas and hopefully undertake improvements in the future.

He has also given us an unprecedented opportunity to truly appreciate what we often take for granted. However, we can still maintain and even improve relationships and communication by the means available to us. Our prayer, though likely different, can be deeply spiritual and move us to deepen our relationship with Hashem and with others.

I will continue to search for the "hidden diamonds" in this pandemic, in this unprecedented time in history. For me and, I have no doubt, for many others, deriving deep meaning and useful lessons from this critical period can help us get through these challenges and, hopefully, usher in better—much better—times.

July 24, 2020

Diamond Mining on Planet Corona

Actually, the title of this letter is misleading. There *isn't* any diamond mining on Planet Corona. Not in the conventional sense. But there *are* diamonds. Everywhere. However, one doesn't descend into the bowels of the earth with mining tools to search for them. In any case, even on Earth, the odds of finding a diamond are equal to being struck by lightning on your birthday 20 years in a row! (A tidbit found on Google).

And even if you *did* mine for diamonds in the "usual" manner— there being three modes of diamond-mining—you would need training and experience to know what you were looking for or at. A "diamond in the rough" doesn't resemble the sparkling gem in an engagement ring. *That* diamond has undergone a delicate process of cutting and faceting, undertaken by a well-trained and well-paid expert.

A rough diamond can easily be mistaken for quartz, which is worth only a fraction of "a girl's best friend." One could even say that—considering the lengthy, laborious, and often fruitless process involved in finding, mining, cutting, and finishing a gem-quality diamond—it's more correct to say that diamonds are "made" rather than "found." Of course, the caveat is that you have to have an *actual diamond* to work with.

The difference on Planet Corona is that while diamonds are, indeed, everywhere, they exist largely in the eyes and soul of the beholder. That does not make them any less real or precious. Their "value is far above rubies," but they are often well-disguised, usually very much "in the rough." These diamonds can gleam in people whom you meet or in events that occur. They may exist in a hidden way within the person or experience, or be found alongside them. I have decided that the very best occupation on Planet Corona is to search for, uncover, and polish these gems.

As I said, some of the diamonds are well-hidden and take an effort to uncover. One of these was a short video that was sent to me about new eyeglasses that improve color vision. It begins with a middle-aged man coming out onto his front porch where his family breaks into "Happy Birthday to You." He is then given a gift which he unwraps. It's a pair of eyeglasses. He looks confused, but is told to put them on. When he does, he's in shock and overwhelmed. The subtitles say that he has been color-blind all his life and these glasses correct that. This gruff, wise-cracking man is choked up and literally "can't believe his eyes."

It was a very moving film, but so often what comes over the Internet turns out to be untrue or exaggerated. So I investigated via Google whether these eyeglasses really did what they purport to do, i.e., correct color-blindness. The first site I read said that the claims by the manufacturers were not as dramatic as depicted. When a second friend sent the same video, I wrote to her about these findings.

I then became a little uneasy. Had I become so very cynical and distrusting? It really wasn't like me. So, I investigated further and found a site that showed that the glasses were effective in improving color vision, making colors brighter and more distinct. And I thought to myself, "Isn't that enough?!" Imagine glasses that show you a wider range of colors that are also brighter. Wouldn't that be sufficient for enormous gratitude. It certainly would make one's daily blessing of "Who opens the eyes of the blind" infinitely more meaningful and heartfelt.

I then wrote to my friend and apologized. I realized that it hardly mattered whether or not the video was true or even somewhat exaggerated. The diamond was there. Gratitude for eyesight and for all the elements of it including color, range, and clarity is a diamond. A very large one. Indeed, what blind person would not give the value of a precious jewel for the priceless gift of eyesight.

A second diamond was found, cut, polished, and displayed by someone else. But, once it was placed on display, it became the "property" of everyone who chose to behold it.

Several weeks ago, a video went viral showing a young chareidi* girl being "harassed" by police in Jerusalem for not wearing a mask (the story appears to be that she had just finished eating a slushy) and she was crying, having been told that she was going to be served with a ticket. Many protests and indignant reactions were written and sent out via the Internet and also appeared in the newspapers. Much was said about police insensitivity or even about chareidi non-compliance. It was not a pleasant Planet Corona event.

Shortly afterward, the father of the young girl, a chareidi man who made aliya with his family from America about 12 years ago, wrote a very upbeat, positive, and optimistic blog that appeared in The Times of Israel. His name is Shia Getter and the blog is well worth reading. He wrote of the huge outpouring of sympathy that followed the incident which came from all kinds of Jews, from Israel and from abroad. He received messages from members of Knesset and from the police force.

There were even indications that the police would, in future, receive some sensitivity training. In fact, the photo that accompanied the article showed Getter and his family standing alongside two members of the police force, everyone wearing masks. Properly. What a gleaming, perfectly polished diamond.

These diamonds are truly everywhere. It may take imagination to see the diamond within or alongside someone or something that is not vaguely diamond-like. The way that Avraham saw the Tzelem Elokim within the dirty, idol-worshipping Arab peddlers. The way a mother will detect and nurture the gem-like spark of greatness and purity within a difficult child.

I've looked for and found some smaller, but brilliant diamonds in the last few days. For instance, I hate getting "needled." I always have. It was hard to find the diamond in my recent experience of having a blood test. But it was there, in the person of the very sweet nurse who kept smiling and apologizing for "hurting" me (she really didn't). I've also just had a tooth extracted. (Yes, it hasn't been an easy week for the squeamish). The diamond in that was stubbornly elusive.

But there were some lovely "chips" after all. One was learning to be grateful for having most of my own teeth which rarely give me any problems. Another was the existence of skilled dental surgeons who routinely improve the dental health of their patients.

Obviously, the list is nearly endless. This "diamond mining" reminds me of a book by Miriam Adahan, written many years ago called *It's All a Gift*. In the introduction, she writes about the hiddenness of God: "We can't see God directly. We have to *put forth the effort to intuit His presence in everything that happens to us*, to know with heartfelt certainty that He is here, especially in the midst of darkness."

The diamonds that surround us, which Hashem has embedded in our world for our benefit and growth, are available for all to see, to own, to have enrich our lives. It takes a certain skill to detect and then bring out the full brilliance of each diamond. It is a skill that can be developed with constant practice. Our sojourn on Corona affords us a singular opportunity for developing our "mining" skills.

The diamonds you uncover won't all be Hope diamonds. But they can certainly be flawless and brilliant. And gleam with hope.

* Ultra-Orthodox.

July 28, 2020

Birth Pangs

All right! Which one of you has been entreating a Higher Power to allow you to live in "*interesting times*?!" Raise your hands... Higher... I can't see them... Own up, now!... Aha! There's a hand. There and there. Guards! Take them away and have them *shot*! Wait a minute!... On second thought, perhaps I should ask a follow-up question. Which of you has been praying for the Messiah? Aha, that many!

Did you think that the era of the Messiah's coming would be days of ease and comfort? Nonsense! In fact, the Sages of the Talmud prayed *not* to be around for those extremely trying times to come. The *actual arrival* of the Messiah would be glorious. The "birth pangs of the Messiah?" Not so much.

Recently, I read the following: "The end will be good. It's not good? Then, it's not the end!" So, perhaps we'll rescind the order for execution. After all, we are very likely all in the same boat. We look forward to the distant arrival of a great good. We are, however, frequently much less delighted with the process preceding the attainment of that good.

It's similar to childbirth, which is clearly the reason that our Sages employed that language for the Messiah process. Women wish to have children. However, for many, the months of pregnancy and the actual process of giving birth are less enthusiastically anticipated or experienced.

It began with the decree in Gan Eden that henceforth "in pain shall you (womankind) bear children." It later is manifest in Rivka's cry as she experiences a very difficult pregnancy, "If so, why am I thus?!" Still, the difficulty of child-bearing and of the subsequent child-rearing, do not deter women from desiring children. The "birth pangs" and the anticipated result are inextricably connected. In effect, they are stages of the same process.

Still, it is not easy to be in the middle of the process. These days, very little appears to be normal or usual or even familiar. Recently, my son, who is spending the summer in the US for reasons of *parnassa*,* away from his wife and children in Ramat Beit Shemesh, sent a plea for help to us, his parents. He had Israeli utility and health bills that needed to be paid and didn't know what he was supposed to do with them.

He and his family made aliya only recently and it takes a while to become familiar with the Israeli billing jargon. So we, (that is, my husband) helped him with them. It appeared to me somewhat "unfair" that with all the responsibilities and tension of trying to run a summer day camp in NY under the cloud of corona, that he should also be hit with confusing paperwork. However, as I've previously written, I'm searching for the hidden diamonds here on Planet Corona and I feel that I have found one, even in this incident.

As I've said, we live in confounding and abnormal times. So little is "as it once was." But bills *do* arrive and demand payment. And, strange as it may seem, there is some comfort in that. Because that, at least, is something that we are used to. You can depend on being billed. That hasn't changed. Some of us might think, "Well, if other things had to change, *this*, at least, would be a welcome change. Not being billed would hardly be a bad thing."

But, on second thought, if we stopped being billed, wouldn't it seem that the world was in a *total* free-fall? Benjamin Franklin quipped, "In this world, nothing is certain, except death and taxes." It could make one feel almost grateful for taxes! A certainty. An unchanging rock during chaotic times. Even bills can be (little) diamonds.

I recently heard the term *"shigrona"* meaning the *"shigra"* (routine) of this corona period. The problem is that the "new normal" doesn't last long enough to become routine *or* normal. It changes almost daily. So, many of us try to cling to as many comfortable routines as possible. We dress each day as if we were going out at some point even if we don't. We try to have regular meals (with, perhaps, a tad more snacking!) We stay in touch with friends and family even if the means of doing so have changed. Because there is comfort in regularity and familiarity.

Of course, our religious lives have many unchanging routines that indeed give structure to our day, week, and month. This week will be Tisha B'Av,** and even if there will be differences in the way it will be observed, most of us will undoubtedly spend the day very much as we have in the past. Shabbat is still Shabbat. Its arrival time is dependable, and we usher it in with the same blessings and traditions.

If anything, many of us are investing more time, not less, in relationships. We have more time to spend in prayer, more time to think about how we spend our days, leisure time for reflecting on our lives, both our spiritual and physical existence. And many of us are looking for the "hidden diamonds" in this longer-than-expected experience.

One of the things that I recently started is a "Book of Diamonds" in which I really try to uncover and record some unexpected but positive element in each day's experiences and events. It takes some introspection, creativity, and even inventiveness. But it is worthwhile.

I really believe that people are amazingly resilient and flexible. Most people would not have believed that they could have survived the life challenges from which they *have*, in fact, emerged.

Hashem has endowed us with almost bottomless resources for facing and coping with whatever He sends our way. We need to reach deep inside ourselves to access and utilize our strengths and coping mechanisms. I really believe we can. I pray that I can.

* Livelihood.

** The national day of mourning for the destruction of the two Temples.

Tisha B'Av 5780

For Tisha B'Av Afternoon

Smokey the Bear was "born" a few years before me. He was created by the US Forest Service to be the mascot for a massive effort to prevent forest fires, those that were ignited naturally, e.g., by lightning, but especially ones started by human carelessness. His motto, spoken in stentorian tones, was "Only you can prevent forest fires."

With these dramatic and oft-repeated words, Smokey made a great impression on the American public and, indeed, the incidence of forest fires decreased dramatically. Interestingly, Smokey appeared on the scene shortly after Disney's famous movie, *Bambi,* in which the beloved fawn loses his mother in a raging fire. This also made a deep impression on children. Forest fires were bad!

So, imagine my surprise, when I first began to visit the great US National Parks, to find that forest fires were being deliberately started in several parks by the Forest Service itself! They had discovered that by over-protecting the forests from fire, many forests had become overly dense with trees, which had several unexpected and unwelcome results. For one thing, when fires did occur, they were much more ferocious and damaging than in the past, because there was so much more fuel to sustain the flames.

Also, in the over-thick forests the nearly solid canopy that developed blocked out much of the sun, making it difficult for smaller plants to survive. And since much of forest wildlife depended on these plants, the creatures of the forest also began to disappear. Including Smokey and his family. Bambi, too. In fact, after serious forest fires, the regrowth of other plants and trees and the return of forest animals is assured. What the Forest Service (and I) had discovered is that fires are actually beneficial for proper forest growth.

Sometimes, there needs to be some "death" for life to continue more vigorously, or even for life to continue at all. When a seed is planted, it has to disintegrate before a new plant or tree can emerge. When we reap fruit, vegetables, and grains, we remove them from their source of "life" in order to sustain us and give life to all of Hashem's creations.

There are myriads of examples of this truth. Just as the process of attaining some great good always contains elements of effort, difficulty, and even suffering, similarly, on occasion, destruction must precede rebuilding. In fact, according to the Torah laws of Shabbat, destruction of a wall, or anything else, is only forbidden if the destruction is necessary for subsequent rebuilding.

Which brings us to this saddest of days, Tisha B'Av. We are familiar with the following concept from the Gemara: "Everyone who mourns for Jerusalem merits to share in her joy" (Ta'anit 30b).

Previously, I had always understood this was a reward/punishment paradigm. If one properly mourned, deeply and honestly, the destruction of the Beit Hamikdash, they would be rewarded with sharing in the joy of the Rebuilding of the Temple. And if not, not.

But perhaps it is not a question of reward and punishment. Perhaps it's part of the same process, an inevitable outcome of sorts. Only by properly mourning destruction are you prepared for the joy of rebuilding. It is through an achingly painful sense of deep loss that one is more fully prepared for the joy of return. To the degree that grief carves out a void of emptiness and longing, that is the size of the space that can ultimately be filled with joy and happiness.

We are all deeply aware that the deprivations of our stay on Planet Corona will sharply enhance our pleasure when we can re-experience those people and things we have missed so much. Like the first hug of a grandchild.

It is now the afternoon of Tisha B'Av on Planet Corona. Our tradition says that the Messiah is born at this time. The hope of our *Geula*, our Redemption, begins immediately in the afternoon of *Galut* (exile), of *Churban* (destruction). It has to be this way. There is no other option.

May this Tisha B'Av contain a double "never again." Let this be the last Tisha B'Av that we mourn a destroyed Temple and a diminished Yerushalayim. And may it be our last Tisha B'Av on Planet Corona.

Chapter Six

August 2020

Another Ministry Visit

Once again, I found myself on the way to visit the Corona Government Offices. Actually, I had been "invited," along with nearly all the inhabitants of Planet Corona, to the Coronese Ministry of the Interior to modify our visas. It appears that we were all to change our status from that of "Tourist" to that of "Temporary Resident."

Naturally, there had been some opposition to this move, but the government had not tolerated demonstrations and ones that started were immediately dispersed. Of course, the newspapers *protested* the handling of the *protests*, but the "invitations" remained in effect.

Since so many of us were affected, the government had set up a number of locations where these adjustments could be made. I was assigned to the ministry's main office. I had been prepared to find long lines, but they were far longer than I had envisaged because of the 2-meter distance that had to be maintained between individuals or families.

The notice I had received suggested bringing along reading material, but I noticed that most of the people had not done so. They were either on their cell phones—obviously commiserating

159

with their friends who were also standing in line somewhere—or grumbling loudly. I had brought my latest novel by Jane Austen, who was the chronicler of an era when people didn't do much, rarely traveled, yet somehow kept occupied. It all seemed rather familiar to me, somehow.

Knowing that I would be standing in the summer heat, I had brought along a bottle of water, but others had not had the fore-thought. Fortunately, the ministry had the kindness to provide water to those in line, each bottle with the letters DBA-IDK printed on the labels. I noticed that the people handing out the water were also wearing badges with those letters. I was intrigued, but they seemed too busy and harried for me to ask the meaning of the letters.

When it was my turn to enter the building, I, of course, had my temperature checked. I felt a pang of nostalgia for the days when we only had our *bags* checked at the door. Again, I noted that all the government employees were wearing badges with DBA-IDK on them. They were scurrying about and, frankly, they all looked rather confused and preoccupied and I began to wonder how helpful any of them would prove to be. I was about to discover the answer.

I was directed to a long and slow-moving line for visa changes. To my left, I noticed another line that had formed in front of a plexiglass window with a sympathetic-looking woman sitting on the other side. The sign on the window identified this location as the Office of Customer Relations (i.e., Complaints Dept.) The representative was also wearing the ubiquitous badge and was subject at the moment to a tirade from the woman in front of the window. It was impossible not to overhear her storm of protest.

"But I don't *want* to be *any kind* of resident! Not even tempo-rary. In fact, I am ready to leave *now*! This visit hasn't been at all what I expected! We don't get to see any interesting sites. Any hotel room or vacation apartment is fine when you spend little time in it. But, if you have to be inside for days at a time, the accommoda-tions here leave a *lot* to be desired!"

The woman on the other side of the window kept making sympathetic noises and nodded in commiseration. This did not, however, appease the dissatisfied complainer.

"Oh, sure there's plenty of food, but the menu is getting very boring. And there is too much of it! I can hardly fit into the clothes I brought with me! And all the exercise gyms are closed! And I *hate* jogging in a mask!"

The clerk handed her a list of clothing shops that hadn't yet gone out of business and an exercise video, and called out, "Next."

As my line had only advanced a little, I was able to observe this other queue and noticed that all complaints were handled in a similar way, with the clerk placidly nodding, listening sympathetically, and saying, "Next" as each tirade ended. I realized that complaining would be useless and determined not to do so. As another clerk passed me, I quickly asked him, "Could you tell me what those letters, DBA-IDK, on the badges stand for?"

"Oh," he said, "that's for 'Don't Bother Asking – I Don't Know.' It's the new government slogan. In fact, it's been adopted by all the ministries and at every level. The Ministry of Health has ordered boxes of them. And the Ministry of Information can't get enough. We find that the slogan has really reduced the number of all kinds of inquiries significantly. If you'd like, you can pick up a few free badges on your way out. Some of our residents have found them helpful with family and friends."

I resolved to take a few, as I was sure that they'd come in handy.

By the time I reached the front of the line to get my visa changed, I did so with a sigh of resignation. Obviously, opposition would be of no use and complaining would only yield a sigh and a "Next." If there were any answers, they wouldn't be obtained here. I wasn't even sure anymore what the questions should be.

I'm going to wear my new badge wherever I go. It really appears to sum up our present situation. To a T.

August 10, 2020

2020: Year of Vision

I recently received a collection of humorous memes (I had to doublecheck the meaning of that word to be sure I didn't use it incorrectly and get laughed at!) about our pandemic. It's been a while since I've received any. At the beginning of our stay on Planet Corona, they appeared with great frequency. In the selection I received, there were a few relating to our secular year. One declared: "The dumbest thing I've ever purchased was a 2020 planner." Another inquired querulously, "When Does Season TWO of 2020 Start? I Do Not Like Season ONE!"

I reminded myself that at the end of 2019, realizing that the coming year would have a significant number, i.e., 2020, I wondered what *visionary* element would be uncovered in the coming year. Of course, this association of 2020 with vision is limited to those of us who grew up in the US (Liberia and Myanmar are the only other countries that use the imperial system of feet, inches, etc.). 20/20 refers to normal vision acuity, meaning that one can see at 20 feet what they *should* see at that distance. In the rest of the world, the measure would be 6/6 measured in meters.

But for us, 20/20 eyesight is more than just an optometric measurement. It represents the idea of *vision* in its broadest sense. "2020 Vision," or a variant, has been the name of several music albums, an episode on the TV series *The Twilight Zone*, and visionary programs for the future of cities, countries, and science. It is the slogan for Kanye West's 2020 presidential campaign (you will be wholeheartedly forgiven if you have no idea who he is!).

Perhaps most famously, until now, it was the name of Barbara Walters' long-running news program on ABC where each episode began with her words, "This is 20/20!" In fact, on *Good Morning America* on January 1, 2020, Walters was invited as a guest to usher in the new year with her famous words. Little did she know, or could have known, that her long-running program would take a distant back seat to the *real* legacy of the year 2020 and the undoubtedly long-lasting referential event of this year, namely the pandemic.

All this raises two questions. First, what experiences of vision have we had or are we meant to have on Planet Corona? Second, is there any specific Planet Corona message for those raised or living in the US for whom 2020 has the specific reference to sight and vision?

Beginning with physical eyesight, we can ask, what enhances one's clarity of vision and what elements can blur or detract from visual acuity? Certainly, near-sightedness and far-sightedness are two conditions that affect our ability to see clearly. External conditions such as low-light or overly bright light, hazy conditions, and "obstacles in our way," all impact on our apprehension of our surroundings. Cataracts impede our vision and can seriously damage our sight if not removed.

In a broader, more metaphorical sense of "vision," there are counterparts to the above deterrents to clear sight. Sometimes, we are too close to a situation, too personally involved, and even too prejudiced to have clear and objective comprehension. Conversely, being too distant from the object of our metaphorical "gaze" may keep us from noticing important details that would impact heavily on our comprehending what or who we witness.

Similarly, darkness of all kinds, whether due to some very difficult situation or to our own "dark" emotions, will often color how we view something or someone. But trying to be upbeat and "sunny" at all times and in all situations, especially when the situation is not your own but someone else's, can be off-putting to a friend or family member who is in difficult or painful straits.

We often don't "see" clearly because we project our own feelings, ideas, and prejudices on the other, or on the situation, which definitely can "fog up" our vision.

What of obstacles, or cataracts, which can effectively block or seriously blur our ability to see with acuity? Obstacles are more like temporary obstructions that are situation-specific and only occur occasionally. Cataracts more resemble character traits, strong prejudices, or deeply imbedded sympathies or, more often, *antipathies* that can be permanently or semi-permanently deleterious to one's vision.

When writing about prophets, visionaries, seers, our Sages differentiate between Moses and all other prophets. They describe Moses' prophecy as seeing with an "*aspaklaria me'ira*," a totally clear lens, whereas all other prophets saw with an "*aspaklaria lo me'ira*," an unclear lens.

I would suggest that there is a connection between the statement that Moses was the "most humble of men" and his clarity of vision. It is often our ego, or elements of egoistic preoccupation, that keep us from seeing things as they truly are.

In Chassidic thought, elements of "*yesh*," selfness or ego, are what separate us from being able to totally connect to the Divine and from that vantage point to be privy to Truth. The more "*ayin*," selflessness, within a person, the greater the ability to connect to Hashem and also to one's fellow man.

Moses, in his great humility, had peeled the metaphysical cataracts from his spiritual eyes and saw everything with crystal clarity.

Here on Planet Corona, many of our previous self-centered activities are no longer available. There's much less going to the gym, going out to restaurants, for entertainment, or for recreational pastimes and travel. It is certainly true that, at least at the start of the pandemic, many people tried hard to fill their empty hours with distractions, often frivolous, which left little time for contemplation and observation. But by now, many of these distractions have worn thin.

Without distractions, it's possible that some of us are seeing our reality with more clarity for once. Seeing what's *really* important and of value. We have more free time to develop greater in*sight* and our hind*sight* is, as the saying goes, "always 20/20."

What is the special message in all this for those of us for whom the number 2020 resonates more deeply due to our use of the imperial system of measurement?

America has long been, for its citizens and for people around the world, the epicenter of consumerism. Materialism found its most fertile breeding grounds in the US resulting in large homes, cars, Amazon, bursting clothes closets, gadgets galore, technical toys that were ubiquitous and relatively inexpensive, etc. The successful hero was always the one with the largest bank account, and rags-to-riches stories have long been a staple of American popular reading.

But materialism is the thickest, most opaque cataract that exists. It not only distorts one's vision as to what life is truly for, it can actually blind one to the simplest yet deepest truths.

Of course, materialism did not begin in the US and the unique brand of American materialism has been exported along with Amazon all around the world. But wherever there is over-indulgence and great emphasis on physicality, a barrier is created between our physical and spiritual selves and our comprehension and vision is compromised.

For many of us, this pandemic has helped put physicality in its proper place. We've found that we can survive with fewer trips to the malls, to restaurants, to entertainment and sports events. What we find ourselves longing for are those things that money can't buy: face-to-face interactions with friends and family, hugs, long walks without masks, etc. That's what we see when the fog of physicality is lifted.

This is 2020. A year when we can choose to see more clearly and live more fully, or we can choose to close our eyes to what is truly real and live in denial of our spiritual needs and potential. *U'vchartem b'Chayim* "And you shall choose Life"

August 11, 2020

The "Mask"-erade

It has just been brought to my attention (by myself) that I have written very little about what is certainly the most central and ubiquitous symbol of this pandemic. Namely, the *mask*. It obviously isn't because I haven't noticed, since, short of people who have never gone out, looked out of their windows, or seen television or news media, there isn't anyone on Planet Corona who can have missed the masks, masks, masks, everywhere!

Additionally, I am meticulously careful to wear one (properly, I may add) whenever I am out of my home, and am critical, though not as stridently as some, when I see people not adhering to the legal and health requirements of mask-wearing.

So why have I not devoted more space to writing about this phenomenon? Since I've focused on many elements of our sojourn on Planet Corona, why have I not written about the national costume, namely the mask, in all its forms? I venture to guess that it's because, on some level, I'm *in denial*. I can't deny it. I don't like masks! Not at all.

You can match them to your wardrobe, have them decorated by your granddaughters (I have), wear them with your favorite logos on them (we are now walking advertisements), or have them proclaim messages (I have one that says "Gossip doesn't 'speak' to me"), but I still can't warm to them.

Knowing how important wearing a mask is to my health and to the health of others, why is it that I find it difficult to feel at all positive about these necessary appurtenances? For one thing, I have to admit that when I am out driving and see the usual street scenes that are so familiar except for the fact that *everyone is wearing a mask (!!!)*, I feel as though I'm in an episode of *The Twilight Zone*.

It's terribly disconcerting. I find that my breathing is more labored when my nose and mouth are covered, making walking outdoors much less of a pleasure than it should be when we are so often confined. And masks offer an additional reason to be annoyed with my fellow man who may not be adhering to the law, when I generally have enough reasons for that without this particular issue. Not that I'm proud of that quality of mine, but there it is.

The fact is, I am a devoted "people person" and masks make it very difficult to recognize others on the street or in shops. Let alone converse. Anxious introverts may actually *welcome* the anonymity offered by the masks, but for the extrovert, they represent a serious hindrance to camaraderie and social interaction. And if you are also wearing sunglasses, which in the Jerusalem sun is almost always necessary, it's nearly impossible to identify anyone. Which is great if you are doing something illicit (which explains bank robbers), but isn't so great if you go out amongst people at least partly to see... you know... *people*!

As it happens, someone attempted to deal with this difficulty, and several months ago I received a short video about a European city which had installed special mask-making machines in public places. These took a picture of the lower half of your face and, on the spot, created a mask for you with the imprint of your face on it.

Unfortunately, that meant that the bottom half of your face would be frozen in whatever expression you had on when the camera clicked. Presumably, most people would have been photographed with a smile which could be problematic if you happen to meet a friend on the street who tearfully tells you that he's just lost his job. At best, the frozen face looks rather bizarre.

Perhaps the greatest loss brought about by the masks is the disappearance of the smile. I have found that on the rare occasions when I have been photographed with a mask on, I automatically smile anyway. It feels more as if I am actually having my picture taken. More "normal."

I also continue to smile when I see adorable children and I hope that they sense that I am doing so. Or that their parents recognize that someone finds their offspring charming. But perhaps they don't detect this, and if not, what a loss for us both.

Smiles are among the most bonding of expressions and the mask is an obstacle to the giving and receiving of this show of warmth and humor.

But for the loss of the smile covered by a mask, there is a remedy. A hope that not all is lost. For it appears that we do not smile solely with our mouths, which are unfortunately covered, but also, and more importantly perhaps, with our eyes.

In the 1860s, the French anatomist Benjamin-Amand Duchenne de Boulogne carried out scientific studies to analyze the smile to study how "facial muscles contract to speak the language of the emotions and the sentiments." He found that a sincere "smile of joy" or a "true smile" also involves the eyes. His conclusion was that a "mouth smile" obeys the will, and can consequently be faked, but that the "eye smile" does not. He said, "The muscle around the eye... is only brought into play by a true feeling, an agreeable emotion. Its inertia in smiling unmasks a false friend."

Perhaps the message in that is, remove your sunglasses on occasion so that someone can see that you are smiling even when you are wearing a mask. The eyes, it is said, are the "windows of the soul" and that is a form of communication that we can still practice without incurring a 500 shekel fine.

It's both significant and appropriate that for many of us the *real* corona crisis began on the heels of Purim, the holiday most associated with mask-wearing. In fact, this year I wore a rather elaborate Venetian mask as part of my Purim costume. With it I had on a sign that said, "Don't worry. This mask is not due to Corona. I bought it in Venice 3 years ago." At the time, we thought that was pretty funny. Ha, ha!

However, the themes of hiddenness and revelation relating to times of "*hester panim*"* have threaded their way through the entire pandemic experience. We wonder about hidden messages, wonder where Hashem is, where we are. The entire last five months is a masked period. Perhaps we would do well to look out for the "twinkling eye" of Hashem in all things.

None of us knows how long the wearing of masks will be obligatory or "only" highly recommended. Your guess is as good as mine or anyone else's. Living with masks presents difficulties. But, for the moment, doing without them would likely result in more people becoming ill, some of them seriously. So, we will continue to wear masks.

But let us not give up on communicating in any way that we can with family, friends, and Hashem. Masks or no masks.

---

* Lit. "hiding the face," referring to concealed Divine Providence—not the lack of it, but the concealment of it.

August 21, 2020

From New to Nu?!: Part One

I was reminded recently of the great contrast between our state-of-being and outlook when we were newly arrived on Planet Corona and today, five months later. A friend recalled that back then, shortly before the holiday of Passover, she had actually felt *positive* about an opportunity to prove her resilience as she faced a new challenge, even an adventure.

It appears to me, based on my own experience and also on the cartoons, memes, videos, new songs, and inspirational messages that flooded the Web at that time, that we actually *relished* an opportunity to flex our muscles and exhibit the national solidarity, creativity, and inner resolve that would help us cope with an unprecedented situation and unique challenges.

That was then. As my friend pointed out, it was all *new* at the time. Many of us experienced a frisson of excitement at entering an extraordinary new world. We were determined to prove our mettle and, in fact, we *did*. So, now what? We have gone from "New" to "Nu?!." As in "When do we get out of here?"

It was one thing having a Pesach Seder with just our spouse, or with the nuclear family, or perhaps alone. Indeed, everyone I spoke to had found a grandchildren-less seder much more pleasant than anticipated. But facing the High Holy Days during this pandemic is an entirely new challenge. Traditionally, all Jews, from the very devout to the relatively distant, have understood that these holidays are meant to be spent in the (often crowded) synagogue. And that experience is likely to be highly restricted. So, what now?

We are tired of the masks, distancing, restrictions. We have traversed a summer with little variety, not much recreation, no travel to speak of, and an absence of extended family time. No one, but no one, seems to know what is happening or what the prognosis is for the near, or even distant, future. Whenever we think we see the light at the end of the tunnel, it turns into the headlights of an oncoming train!

As I wrote recently, with a good deal of resignation, we have been compelled to "upgrade" our Planet Corona visas from that of a "tourist" to the status of "Temporary Resident" (with a fervent hope for the "temporary!") Yet how do we proceed from here? Now that our status has changed, what adjustments do we need to make to help us survive and hopefully thrive during the upcoming time period?

As I noted above, we've previously gone from "New" to "Nu?!" *Now*, we need to go from "Nu?!" to "New." Not backwards, in some nostalgic movement, to the earlier days of the pandemic. Because you really can't "go home again." But rather forward to a new "New" just as we have been trying to adjust to the "new normal." But this can't be *just* an adjustment. It needs to be an inspired, creative, and active state of being and mode of action. *It doesn't just happen.* It takes effort and determination. But it will be worth it.

As the Torah is returned to the Ark on Shabbat we say a prayer "Turn us back, O Lord to You, and we will return. Renew our days as of old." We are not petitioning to be taken back to some "good old days." Rather, we ask to be taken *forward* to a time and place where, while we are saturated with our entire history to date, we can yet feel the *re-newed* excitement, anticipation, and inspiration that we felt once. When it was first new. Moreover, in each morning's tefillot we praise Hashem, saying, "Lord of wonders, who in His goodness, continually *renews* the work of creation, day after day." Each day is *re-newed*.

"Our days" are renewed. And the work of creating is renewed. While "new" is an adjective, "to renew" is a verb. In fact, it is a transitive verb, meaning that the subject affects something or someone else. Hashem, as it were, *makes* each day new. *It doesn't just happen.*

Similarly, the word "love" can be a noun or a verb. A person can be "in love." which suggests floating in some delicious, or unfortunately sometimes painful, emotional state. Not *doing* anything in particular, just *being*. But even as a verb, "to love" can be stative or dynamic. As a stative verb, it once again indicates a state of being, or an emotion that one is experiencing. The object of that emotion or state is almost secondary.

But, as a dynamic verb, "to love" requires acting on someone else. The object of affection is made to feel the love through action by the lover. Through words of endearment, kind deeds, compassionate and loving gestures, one conveys love to the beloved. *Love doesn't just happen.*

The element of freshness in any relationship must also be constantly nurtured and renewed. To avoid staleness, you have to work on your connections to others. While it's very pleasant to experience a comforting contentment within a long-term relationship, the connective tissue between people needs reinforcement, revitalizing, and reinvigoration. In a word, "*renewal.*"

So, how shall we achieve the "re-newed" state necessary for a fruitful, positive, and protracted stay on Planet Corona? I believe that it calls for a three-pronged approach that can be proposed as Appreciation, Adaptation, and Elevation. There may also be a fourth prong, Resignation.

Prong 1: Appreciation

It helps to focus on some of the unexpected benefits many have experienced. Last week, I participated in a Jewish day-school reunion of some of the girls in my 8th-grade class in Hartford, Connecticut. One of us was in Boca Raton, another in Paris, and two of us were in Jerusalem. It was delightful and only possible because of Zoom which I had never even heard of prior to the pandemic.

Recently, a friend told me that she has been using her extra free time to peruse and sort through the treasure trove of letters dating from the first years of her aliya, more than forty years ago. They were from her mother and mother-in-law who were both living in the US at that time. She smiled as she spoke of the wonderful memories those letters evoked.

I also have to thank the pandemic for summoning forth the (seemingly) hidden writer within me. I had never before thought to write as much or as frequently as I have. And the idea of publishing my writings, which only began to occur to me after having written a number of my Letters, would never have entered my imagination in the past. This opening up of a heretofore closed world is something I am very grateful for.

This approach of Appreciation, otherwise known as "the attitude of gratitude" enhances our lives and, while it has to be *actively* searched for and brought into the light, it is well worth the effort. It brings renewal. And, *it doesn't just happen!*

August 28, 2020

From Nu!? To New: Part II

Last night, I went to India. I must admit that, unlike many Israelis, travelling to India has never been particularly high on my "bucket list." Somehow, riding on the back of an elephant watching the unfortunate (and often maimed) beggars down below, a scene once described by a traveler, isn't my idea of a pleasant vacation.

Nevertheless, with this pandemic keeping us close to home and having wreaked havoc with any and all travel plans for the last half year, going *anywhere at all* has great attractions. Even if the travel is virtual and the scenery is viewed on my computer screen. Which brings me to the second prong of a positive approach to an extended sojourn on Planet Corona.

Prong 2: Adaptation

We all have practiced this to some degree. Some of us have begun shopping in less crowded places, e.g., a makolet vs. a supermarket, attending classes, meetings, even family gatherings via Zoom or other venues rather than in person, working from home rather than going to one's workplace, and many other adaptations.

Sometimes, we've resented and bemoaned these adjustments. However, even according to evolutionary theory, adaptability leads to survival. It is the species that is successful in adapting itself to changing circumstances that survives for another day, generation, or millennium.

You may not be aware of it, but resilience, of which adaptability is an important element, is currently seen as a pillar of positive mental health and of well-being. Resilience training workshops have entered the workplace and are promoted by many mental health professionals. The benefits of increased resilience include lowered levels of depression, reduced sickness-related absence from work, and increased self-esteem. As the SAHMRI Wellbeing and Resilience Centre of Australia puts it:

> Being resilient doesn't mean you won't experience adversity, but having resilience can buffer the adverse effects of stressful life events. Individuals who use a broader range of coping strategies experience less distress from stressful life events.

And, as if these benefits of the resilience training opportunities with which this pandemic has presented us weren't sufficient reason for gratitude, greater resilience can help us *live longer*. An important study showed:

> Resilience significantly contributes to longevity at all ages, and it becomes even more profound at very advanced ages. These findings indicate that policies and programs to promote resilience would have long-term and positive effects on the well-being and longevity for senior citizens and their families.

So, thank you, coronavirus pandemic. However, never forget that *it doesn't just happen!*

Prong 3: Elevation

Has anything been "made better" due to this period on Planet Corona? Well, at the very least, our appreciation of the things that we've formerly taken for granted has certainly increased. We no longer undervalue the "freebies" such as hugs, face-to-face talks, guests at the Shabbat or holiday table, large and pleasant family gatherings, etc. If we can hold on to our new and deeper under-standing of what "really counts" when this is all over, we will have gained immeasurably from the experience.

Certainly, many of us have been given a gift of more "activity-free" time that could be used for improving our minds, marriages, prayers and religious practices, and myriads of other aspects of our lives. If we haven't merely been *marking time*, but rather have been employing our time creatively and positively, we may have achieved a level of personal growth that will impact our lives from now on, whether we are still inhabiting Planet Corona or not.

As the *Yamim Noraim* (the High Holidays) approach, we *could* face them mournfully and lament all the "losses" that are largely inevitable this year. Services will likely be abbreviated, some of us will find ourselves praying in the privacy of our homes, and meals will be smaller, with familiar faces absent. However, that doesn't necessarily mean that our experience need be inferior. There are opportunities to actually improve our customary experience of this time of year.

With more unoccupied time, we can delve more deeply into the meaning of these days and into the prayers themselves. I recently purchased a new set of *mahzorim** with commentary to enhance my tefillot. My husband and I have begun a daily study of a book on Rosh Hashana from Yeshivat Har Etzion. So many books and guides exist that everyone can find something that suits them.

There are so many opportunities now to revisit our usual ways of doing things and see if they can be improved, not just here on Planet Corona but anywhere we find ourselves in the future. But, once again, any improvement in this area *doesn't just happen*. And this brings me to the fourth "prong."

Prong 4: Resignation

It occurs to me that this is less a "prong" than the body of the "fork" which helps us "handle" (sorry) the entire situation with greater serenity and positivity. It would perhaps be more proper to call it "Acceptance" rather than "Resignation." We are here on Planet Corona and we don't know the duration of our stay.

We can try to forget that we are here, as some do, but it doesn't change the reality. We can flout the rules of the planet, but we have already seen where that leads. We can live on Planet Denial but, frankly, that's a much more inhospitable planet than Corona.

So, we are left with only one rational option. That is to resign ourselves to, or accept, our present circumstances and use the three-pronged approach to making this stay both productive and positive, helping us develop resilience, flexibility, deeper understanding, and personal growth. Which can and will occur as long as we remember that *it doesn't just happen!*

* High Holiday prayer books.

August 31, 2020

Driving Us Mad on Planet Corona

Once again, I'm on my way to a Corona government office. This time, however, my destination is the Department of Motor Vehicles. All drivers have been summoned to have a high-tech program installed in their vehicles. We each have to bring our licenses with us to a preliminary orientation explaining the purpose and function of the new program. Then, we have a week to bring our vehicles to one of the special service centers to have the program installed.

Some people I know may need to search for their licenses as they haven't needed them for months. Obviously, enough people have located them, as the lines at the department offices are rather long. Which doesn't surprise me.

What *does* pique my curiosity is that the department employees and officers now are wearing two badges. One says DBA-WDK which, I discovered on my last visit to a ministry, stands for "Don't

Bother Asking – We Don't Know." However, the additional badge says BTO-WND. I try to puzzle out the meaning for myself and notice that others standing in line are attempting to decipher it also.

A woman in the line, Shira, with whom I've been chatting, tells me that she is a high-school teacher and recognizes one of the employees as a former student. She collars him, and after exchanging pleasantries (masked, of course), inquires into the meaning of the second badge. He reveals that the letters stand for "But That's Okay – We Never Did." Shira and I smile at each other. Humility in a government office. And on Planet Corona, no less. How very unexpected!

We are admitted into the orientation room six at a time to allow for appropriate social distancing. I notice that there is a sprightly tune playing on the loud-speaker system, but I can't catch the words. In any case, there is no time to listen more carefully as my group has just been admitted for the orientation.

As soon as we are seated, a pleasant-looking woman comes into the room and begins to address us. She begins by introducing herself as "Lolo" Yoda'at* (obviously a nickname for "Leah." Interesting how even high-ranking officials here are known almost solely by nicknames. Bibi, for instance.) She then proceeds to present the new program.

"Good morning, everyone. You've been gathered here to learn about our new high-tech development that will be installed in all vehicles within the week. We are justifiably proud of our reputation as a Start-up Nation (ed. note: Better than "up-starts" which is an opinion commonly held!), and we now have a form of "driverless car" that we are introducing here."

There are excited murmurings in the (limited) audience. We had no idea they were so close!

"Of course," she continues, "there *are* a few twists to the previous understanding of what a driverless car would be like. For one thing, *you* will still be the drivers."

Murmurings in the audience of "What!?!"

"That is why you were asked to bring a current driver's license. The twist is that *you* will do the actual driving. You won't, however, always determine the destination. That will be determined by the program. It's a sort of reverse Waze. As usual, you will enter your destination which our new program will treat as a *strong suggestion.* You will then choose from several routes to get there.

"As you travel, the program *may*, on occasion, introduce detours, dead ends, and other means of changing direction that might affect where you actually end up." She pauses for a moment. "Now, won't that make things much more exciting? What surprises will be in store for you," she ends cheerily.

Our extremely dubious looks seem to disconcert her for a moment, although, undoubtedly, she had met similar reactions earlier. For the moment, most of us are shocked into silence.

Shira, who has partly recovered the power of speech, shoots her hand up and asks, "Does that mean that we will *never* know where we will end up?"

"No, no," Lolo assures us. "You will *often* end up where you expected. As I said previously, the program will take your wishes into consideration. It's just that you won't be *certain* of your actual destination. That's all."

Clearly hoping that she has appeased us somewhat, she continues: "As you know the advancements in the development of driverless cars derive from progress in the area of 'AI', Artificial Intelligence. We call our foundational basis, 'HI', Higher Intelligence. In fact, this technology has been named, 'The Anochi Program' as in I = Anochi."

She looks around to see if we have "gotten the point" and then concludes by saying, "Our Research and Development Department has expressed great hopes that the widespread use of this program will lead to A Better Tomorrow. Are there any further questions?"

I ask if the program is mandatory, even though I suspect the answer even before she responds that it is. Not only private vehicles will be affected, the program also covers taxis, vans, trucks, buses, trains, planes (See Letter #42, "Planet Corona as Holland), and ships (e.g., the *Titanic*).

We all emerge from the orientation room rather stunned. The same catchy song is still coming over the loudspeakers. This time I catch the words:**

> You never know where you're going, 'til you get there,
> You don't know your destination, 'til you arrive,
> You set off for some place
> And drive at a steady pace,
> But wonder where you will end up, as you drive.
> Oh, you never know where you're going, 'til you get there
> But, as you arrive, be grateful you're alive.

Humming the catchy tune, I walk to my car and drive home. I get there, too.

* Play on words. In Hebrew, "I don't know."
** Sung to the tune of "How do you solve a problem like Maria" (From *The Sound of Music*).

Chapter Seven

September 2020

Picking Yourself up Once Again

There are times when it is difficult to avoid the conclusion that Corona can be a very inhospitable planet. Today is one of those days. I had begun what I intended to be an uplifting and inspirational letter, befitting these days of Elul and the pre-Rosh Hashana period we are in. But I've put that letter on hold in order to take a detour, a short one I hope, to give vent to the less hopeful and non-uplifting feelings of the day.

It's not that the harshness isn't always here on an ongoing basis. I am very aware that there are people suffering physically, financially, psychologically, and emotionally because of this pandemic. Within our own four walls, we have been very fortunate. Much more so than many others. But as the universal and local upheaval keeps seeping in, its effects are cumulative. So that, if you don't want to explode at some point, you must periodically vent and allow some of the built-up frustration and pain to escape.

Someone very dear to me dissolved into tears on the phone last night. She is one of the strongest women I know. But, at present, she is not only overwhelmed by the pandemic as we all are, but she is also absorbed by a personal family health crisis unconnected to Covid-19. (Yes, there are, indeed, other things

179

occurring on the planet.) She understood that her tears were a safety valve that permitted her to remain sane and effective the rest of the time.

So, sometimes we have to let ourselves feel the anguish, the confusion, and the terrible doubts that always threaten to plague us. For otherwise they will collect and overwhelm us. And after we've allowed ourselves to feel and hurt and react, we can pick ourselves up and go on.

I heard a beautiful story recently about Racheli Fraenkel, the courageous mother of one of the three teenaged boys killed by Arab terrorists in 2014. The police had restored a phone call from one of the boys while they were being kidnapped and asked if she wished to hear it. She knew that she would, ultimately, listen to it but she went to a very caring psychologist to help her prepare emotionally for the experience.

> He asked her, "Okay, Racheli, what are you afraid of?"
> She replied, "I'm afraid that I'll fall apart."
> "So, you fall apart. Then what?" he continued.
> "I guess I'll collect myself and get back up," she told him.
> She continued, "I learned that sometimes it's the fear that's worse than actually living through the reality."

We've been hit very hard in the five Cs. Our *comfort* has been disturbed. The familiar *conventions* have all been altered. The *confidence* we've placed in leaders and in our situation is shattered. The *customary* life we once knew, is no longer recognizable. And *conveniences* that we once took for granted, are now rare luxuries. And so we are left with two more Cs—confusion and consternation.

What to do? We are experiencing many adverse effects of this period in history. How do we react? Rabbi Yitzchak Hutner, ztz"l, former head of Yeshiva Rabbi Chaim Berlin responded to a letter from a former student who was despondent over the serious spiritual struggles he was facing. R. Hutner wrote the following:

The wisest of all men [King Solomon] said [Proverbs 24:16], "The tzaddik will fall seven times and will rise." The unlearned think that this means, "Even though a tzaddik falls seven times, he will rise." The wise know well that the meaning is: "*Because* a tzaddik falls seven times, he will rise"… If you had written to me of your mitzvot and good deeds, I would have said that it was a good letter. Now that you tell me of your falls and stumbles, I say that I have received a very good letter.

After we've wept, cried out, felt depressed, worried, complained, or had a meltdown, we have to get up and go on. We'll be better, stronger, more resilient, and somewhat greater for having gone through the experience of despair leading to development, fear giving way to fortitude, sorrow that ends up strengthening, and tears that water the tenacity and resilience that can result from our experiences on Planet Corona.

> Shake yourself off, arise from the dust!
> Put on your clothes of glory…
> Wake up, wake up,
> For your light has come: rise, shine!"

(From the Friday night Sabbath prayers)

September 9, 2020

The Gravity of the Situation

On Planet Corona, many things operate in the strangest ways. All right. Perhaps that is a huge understatement! But I want to focus on one of the strangest. Gravity. Yes, it appears that gravity on Planet Corona is actually *optional*. At least, its *force* is adjustable. By choice. In other words, an individual on the planet can determine the degree to which Coronian gravity either holds them down or allows them "to fly." We have a choice to be either dragged down or uplifted by the planet's gravitational force.

This can be illustrated by two popular local activities with which we may be familiar. When I was (much) younger, there was a craze called the Limbo. It consisted of a bar (often a broom handle) held at each end. The participants would try to get under the bar by bending backwards and walking underneath. If you were limber and had a very supple body, you could bend backwards lower and lower as the bar was brought closer to the ground after each round.

There were hit songs that accompanied this game. One of them, Chubby Checker's "Limbo Rock," contained the following lyric "How *low* can you *go*?!" In the game, those words were an incentive to keep trying to get "lower and lower." The winner of the game was the one who bent lowest.

Because of the "optional" nature of Coronian gravity, the limbo game here reaches extremes of "lowness." Limbo participants can choose to achieve lows that even the most limber of my classmates couldn't replicate.

On the other hand, Planet Corona Olympic athletes have attained unimaginable records in the high-jump event. Because you yourself choose the degree of pull that keeps you earthbound, you find that you can choose to launch yourself to great heights with enhanced success.

Once you've made the choice to leave the ground and soar, you find that you *can* and *do*. And the bar keeps being raised higher and higher. New records are set constantly.

So, you choose whether to "lower" or "raise" yourself. And you use the gravity of Planet Corona to do so. We're all here on the same planet. But we decide whether we're playing Limbo or doing the high-jump. And the results are all around us to witness.

We see residents of Corona choosing to be *lowered* by "the gravity of the situation." Here, "How *low* can you *go*?!" is not an encouragement to them, but a reaction of shock at their actions. Their choice to allow the challenges of the pandemic to overwhelm them sadly results in divisiveness, selfish and dangerous behaviors, and even in violence.

One consequence of their actions is that it sets off an unexpected effect of Coronian gravity which is to shrink their stature. This, despite the fact that what they wished for was to have their own egoistic desires and needs met, even at a high cost to others. But it's a choice they are making. A free choice. They are not *compelled* by circumstances. They choose.

Then there are other residents who are rising to the occasion. They achieve and exhibit heightened levels of charity, kindness, selfless behaviors, and humanity. Same planet. Same gravity. But they have chosen, freely, to use the gravity as a boost to their own character development and growth and for the benefit of others. They are getting larger and larger, although that was not their motivation. And they are not compelled by circumstance either. They also choose.

Make no mistake. Although the planet's gravity can be adjusted by individual choice, it cannot be done away with. There persists a gravitational pull earthward. It's like a down escalator. Without exerting against the downward force, you will inevitably be drawn to lower and lower levels. It's just that if you also walk or even run *down* the escalator, you'll fall faster.

Similarly, upward motion is *also* like being on a down escalator. Therefore, great exertion is necessary to rise step after step against its movement. You must climb determinedly upwards against the gravitational pull so that you can rise higher and proceed faster. But you have to keep moving and growing and developing so that you continue your upward movement and experience few "downs."

There is a popular Coronian fable that is much beloved by the local children, and retained in the memories of the older population. It's entitled, "Two Seeds Sitting in the Sun" and deals with the mysteries of challenge and growth. I have added it at the end of the letter for the benefit of those who may not have had Coronian upbringings.

But the message of the tale is clear. Growing pains may not be pleasant, but without them, even if they may be excruciating at times, there is no growth. There may even be stagnation and decay.

So, there's your choice as a resident of Planet Corona. Limbo or high-jump. Lower the bar or raise it. Diminution or growth. Selfish or helpful. Finding our lowest common denominator as humans or attempting to rise to the heights of human potential. And this pre-Rosh Hashana period is the perfect time to think about this and act on it. Your choice of sporting events will be judged.

TWO SEEDS SITTING IN THE SUN

Two apple seeds lay basking in the summer sunshine on the floor of the orchard. Their names were Benny and Bingo. (Why not?) The day was warm and lazy, and they were very, very, comfortable. But Benny kept looking at the apple trees around him, with their branches forming a canopy overhead. He envied their stout brown trunks, their profusion of bright green leaves, and, most of all, their multi-colored, ripening fruits.

"It must be wonderful being an apple tree," Benny sighed.

"Probably a lot of work," Bingo retorted. "Much nicer just lying here in the sun without effort. Besides, I don't know what it takes to *be* a tree. And, what's more, I don't want to know!"

"All the same," said Benny, "they are very handsome, and I think it must be so nice to make apples that humans like so much."

"Humph," Bingo exclaimed scornfully, "like *I* should do the work and *they* get the fruit! Nope. No way."

Benny decided to drop it. It was too pleasantly warm to get into a heated discussion. Still, he kept thinking of how nice it would be… and he fell asleep.

Next thing he knew a giant human (a five-year-old) picked him up and looked at Benny carefully. The human picked up a thick twig, dug a hole, dropped Benny in, and covered the frightened seed with dirt.

"Well," said Bingo to himself after witnessing the action, "bye-bye Benny. A tree?! Not!"

In the meantime, Benny couldn't see a thing. No longer did he feel the warming rays of the sun or feel the delicate breeze or smell the fragrant fruit.

"Oh, dear," he cried. "What's to become of me?"

Benny was dreadfully lonely. Bingo hadn't been a brilliant conversationalist, but he had been some sort of companion. Benny could only think of Bingo sunning himself and feeling pretty fortunate to have escaped Benny's own fate.

In a few days, things got worse. Benny found himself actually falling apart. His comfortable coat was ripping at the seams and he felt very queasy. "I must be very ill," thought Benny. "I wonder if I'm dying!" He had heard about dying and it had sounded extremely unpleasant. "Will I know when I'm dead?" he wondered fearfully.

Benny felt worse and worse and soon thought that he must really be dead because he knew that there was nothing of himself that was left as it had been. And then, one day, he felt something stirring within him. He was actually *growing*. He knew it because he could feel himself pushing against the dirt that covered him. There were parts of him spreading out to the sides and other parts pushing upwards until, eventually, he felt the warmth of the sun again and realized that he had emerged from the ground.

"Whoa!" Benny exclaimed enthusiastically. "I wonder whether Bingo can see me. What would he say now?" (The answer is "Nothing" because Bingo was long gone. But this isn't his story. It's Benny's.) Benny soon realized that he was actually growing into an apple tree. His dream was coming true. Here he had thought he was *dying*. Instead he was *becoming*. How was that for a surprise!

And so, dear children, (and the grown-ups you will become), don't forget what Benny learned:

"*Out of suffering have emerged the strongest souls; the most massive characters are seared with scars.*"– Khalil Gibran

"*A hero is an ordinary individual who finds the strength to persevere and endure in spite of overwhelming obstacles.*"– Christopher Reeve

"*I really believe in the old expression that what doesn't kill you makes you stronger. It's through adversity that you find the strength you never knew you had.*"– Christie Brinkley

I don't think Benny would have put it quite that way. But, after all, he *was* just a seed!

September 11, 2020

No News Is Good News

It's happened again. I'm in the midst of writing a new letter (or at least I'm mulling it over in my head and writing notes), but then some news or event or dire prognosis interferes and I put the intended letter aside to write something different. Something more pressing that needs to emerge so that I (or perhaps we) can obtain some relief.

And it doesn't seem to matter that I purposely try to ignore all news outlets. For one thing, it doesn't work. It appears that once news is out there somewhere, it permeates everywhere and into everyone. Besides, the news, good or otherwise, need not enter via the news media. It can come in through a phone call, a casual conversation, an overheard comment, etc.

We are beset by fears and worries over what the coming weeks will bring in terms of closures, severe limitations on holiday prayers, additional illnesses, quarantines, and a general unease about the future. Additionally, many of us are being personally affected by the wide spread of the pandemic and, if not personally, we all, with very few exceptions, have children, grandchildren, and other close family who are so affected.

We find ourselves worrying, with good cause, over the present situation and also about the long-term effects, particularly on the young, of this prolonged crisis.

And it's Erev Shabbat, and also one week until Rosh Hashana, and we wish to be using our resources to enter more fully into the preparations for this crucial and urgent period of reflection, repentance, and return. Instead, we seem to be almost paralyzed by the *other* period we are in, that of the Covid-19 epidemic.

We are overwhelmed by the unprecedented and chaotic circumstances of our lives on Planet Corona. We wonder just what this awesome and soul-shaking period of Elul and the High Holy Days is supposed to look like on Planet Corona. We've never been here before at this time. We're on foreign soil and are attempting to understand the local customs and language because, though we will look for the familiar and customary, it's going to be *different*. In many ways. Inevitably. And who is there to guide us and show us the way? We are all newcomers here.

Perhaps we can receive some guidance from the fact that we are about to enter the final Shabbat before Rosh Hashana, the last intimate and loving encounter with Hashem before we stand before Him in judgement and proclaim Him as our King.

For me, although the days of the rest of the week have largely lost their distinctiveness, Shabbat has continued to stand out with its special prayers, meals, and even mode of dress. It is, as it always has been, a day spent more clearly in Hashem's presence with an accent on spirituality, study, and deeper thought.

A friend wrote me today that our actions and speech on this Shabbat carry increased importance. The day affords us an opportunity to exhibit our understanding of and commitment to the way Shabbat is *supposed* to be spent. We can and should be kinder, more thoughtful, more introspective, with increased gratitude, inner serenity, and trust in Hashem.

And just as we add onto the 24 hours of Shabbat both before it enters and at the point of its departure, so we can begin our improved actions and words prior to the onset of Shabbat and carry them forward even after she departs.

This Shabbat has an interesting feature, or rather the feature is notably absent. On the Shabbat before a Rosh Chodesh we proclaim and bless the upcoming month. Although Rosh Hashana is simultaneously Rosh Chodesh Tishrei, the beginning of the month of Tishrei, we do not make the usual proclamation and blessing. Several reasons are given for this anomaly.

The Ba'al Shem Tov teaches that we don't bless the New Moon of Tishrei because *God Himself* blesses Tishrei—and with the power God invests in the month of Tishrei, we have the ability to bless the other 11 months of the year. It means that even before judging and evaluating us on Rosh Hashana, Hashem is already bestowing His own blessing on us in the month of Tishrei and throughout the coming year! Would that we could enter into any *earthly* court of law knowing that the judge is *totally on our side!*

In the way that a parent may watch a child facing challenges and be cheering him on all the while, so our Father is rooting for us to be successful even if it is He who has posed the challenges. It's like teachers who test their students. They want them to be successful. But they don't make the tests overly easy , nor do they provide them with the answers.

What they do is prepare them for the exams, make sure that the questions are challenging enough so that the students can feel a sense of well-earned accomplishment, and, all the while, silently cheer them on.

Have a wonderful Shabbat.

September 16, 2020

A Letter to Me

(Today, *I myself* received a letter from Planet Corona. It was unexpected and it was addressed to me and meant for me. But I think it's worth sharing with you, particularly in this week before the strangest Rosh Hashana that most of us have ever faced. So, here it is.)

Dear Chaya,

Good morning. I am aware that you are presently going through some difficult times. Aren't we all? Especially now, with the holiest days of the year approaching and no certainty even yet of how these days will play out. Still not sure where and how you will pray or hear the sounds of the shofar. Not certain if you will be able to entertain or be hosted even in a limited way. With all the uncertainty that has existed until now, this period is adding still another opaque layer of questions, discomfort and groping in the dark.

But you've been one of those who have been aware, almost from the start, that we are on a foreign planet, an alien and unexplored area, very different from what we've known heretofore. It was you who dubbed our new address, Planet Corona, and have been pointing out its positive features and its difficult challenges.

You've been exploring the planet and its inhabitants for months now. So then, nothing really has changed. It's simply that we are continuing to discover elements of Planet Corona of which we were unaware until now.

Of course, you never imagined, seven months ago, that we would be facing a Tishrei still on this planet. None of us did. Pesach was one thing. But Rosh Hashana, Yom Kippur, and Sukkot?! That's quite another thing entirely.

Still, one realization that you have always maintained is that we are most definitely *not in charge* of events! So, this eventuality *always* existed. We just hadn't imagined it *actually happening*. But then, we never imagined, or could have imagined, any of this.

I've also been made to understand that some of your difficulties emerge from the fact that you are feeling the pain of others, many in your own family, whose lives are being so heavily affected by the pandemic. And you've previously told me that what makes this "second-hand pain" sometimes harder to withstand than your own difficulties is the fact that you can't arm against it.

You can't say "It's all for the best" when it's someone's else's affliction. Nor can you take comfort in the hope that it will make you stronger, more resilient, closer to Hashem, or closer to others. Because it's not about you now. It's about someone else. And you can't rationalize for anyone else. But there is only one address for your pain and prayers. And you know what It is.

A close friend of mine (of yours, too) has been teaching us lately from *Chovot Halevavot* (*Duties of the Heart*) by Rabbi Bachya ibn Pakuda. One of the recent lessons taught is that in order to serve Hashem with joy, an important element is appreciation. We need to become more aware of the countless blessings which we so often take for granted—the intricate and interconnected workings of the natural world, our unimaginably complex bodies and minds, even the miracles of world events.

Furthermore, to maintain positive relationships with others, we need to appreciate all their positive characteristics and the commonalities we share, and not focus on the blemishes and on our differences. And one of the "others" we need to appreciate more is… ourselves!

Especially in these sober days of repentance, and on Planet Corona at that, while we work towards a clarifying analysis of our faults and mistakes, we must not forget our positive traits and good deeds. Otherwise, we could be plunged into a depression that would not result in repentance, but rather in paralysis. Remember that Rabbi Akiva's "great principle of the Torah" of "Love your neighbor as yourself" only works if you do, indeed, love yourself.

So, as a good and loving friend, I suggest that you view your empathy as a potentially good and even laudatory trait that must, however, be used positively and wholesomely. Don't let it overwhelm your joy and gratitude for all the blessings that you have. It's another of the challenges of life in general and on Planet Corona in particular. It's all a part of the "life" that we were exhorted "to choose" in last week's parsha.

I'd like to suggest that you reach out to the people who read your letters and encourage them to view this New Year as a fresh opportunity for growth in gratitude, in developing relationships, in deepening their spirituality, and in appreciating others and themselves. Talk to them about Life. Why not title it "To Be Alive"?

One of your best friends (I know you have others. Lucky you!)

K'Tiva V'Chatima Tova

September 18, 2020

To Be Alive

If bungee jumping, skydiving, extreme sports, or other life-threatening activities appeal to you, then you are in for a disappointment. They just don't happen on Planet Corona. None. Nada. And if you object to the term "life-threatening," and point out that driving a car is far more dangerous, that may be statistically true.

But you don't drive a car solely for the thrill of putting your very life on the line (well, not unless you drive on Route 6 in Israel!) but *that* is the totality of the allure of those extreme activities.

Studies have shown that people engage in these life-on-the-line pursuits because, in facing death or serious injury they experience a strong adrenaline rush to which they sometimes become addicted. By facing and escaping death, though they've done so willingly (and perhaps paid rather heavily for the privilege), they experience exhilaration and feel more "alive."

Therefore, it's no surprise that, as 20th- and 21st-century life became safer, more comfortable and potentially duller, these activities grew rapidly in popularity. When your life is plodding, perhaps too safe, and relatively uneventful, it appears that people look to *artificially* make life more exciting.

Not needed here on Planet Corona. There's enough excitement, eventful days, and *true* life-threatening circumstances to satisfy the most addicted adrenaline junkie. We are alive, on a daily basis, to the fact that life is tenuous and survival is not guaranteed. No need to pay large sums to have your life threatened. We now know that life is constantly on the line. Your health, relationships, income, education, and even the state of your political life are tenuous and out of your personal control.

So, our adrenaline needs are being amply supplied. But is that Life? Is our time on earth meant to be viewed as an ongoing "Perils of Pauline" where we are brought to the brink and rescued countless times? When Moshe Rabbeinu exhorts us to "Choose life!" does anyone believe that this is what he had in mind?

During the 1964–1965 World's Fair in Flushing Meadow NY, a short and innovative film was introduced at the Johnson's Wax Pavilion. It became very popular and ultimately won an Oscar. It was titled *To Be Alive*. I remember seeing it then as a teenager and remember that I loved it.

The film opens with frenzied scenes of the "rat race" of "making a living." At that point, the narrator says, "But is that *living*?" There's a pause, the tempo slows, and the film proceeds to the joys of growing up, of discovery, of building lasting relationships, and of the simple and pure joys of living. The point is that the film begins with the rush of modern city life, takes a deep breath, and then explores alternative ways of looking at life.

So, what have *we* learned about life this year? Well, some of us have suggested, semi-seriously, that we would have preferred to totally miss the last seven months. There were mock ads for "YearQuil – Hybernate," a pill that would help you "sleep until 2021." But you never would have been able to sleep through 2020, even had you tried this fictional product. There were too many rude awakenings.

In any case, we are in the period of the "wake-up call" of the shofar, on the brink of Rosh Hashana and the Ten Days of Repentance. Maimonides says that the shofar blasts should be heard as an alarm clock that blares out the message, "Wake up, you slumbering ones!" We ask for life for the coming year. We address Hashem saying, "Remember us for life, O King who desires life, and write us in the book of life – for Your sake, O God of life." What is it we are asking for so repeatedly?

On a very basic level, we ask to be given another year of physical existence. Another year to enjoy the fruits of the earth, our human relationships, our physical pleasures. Our bodies are miraculous and complex mechanisms and our gratitude for the largely well-oiled operation of our bodies and minds should be a source of immense gratitude for us.

Stephen Hawking was a brilliant physicist and thinker who was struck with ALS in his early twenties when he was told he had two more years to live at the most. In the end, he lived for 50 more years, married, had three children, wrote numerous books and articles, and received many awards and titles. He lost all powers of voluntary movement early in his illness and, shortly after, he lost the power of speech and only spoke with an artificial, mechanical voice.

In a movie made about his life, there is a scene in which he is delivering a lecture and notices that someone has dropped a pen. The film freezes and Hawking, in his imagination, begins to regain the power of his muscles, steps off the stage, walks over to where the pen is on the floor, stoops to pick it up, and returns it to the owner. One of the most brilliant minds of our century, and what he envies in others are the simple movements that we certainly take very much for granted!

But there's more to our lives than the physical and intellectual pursuits that are enabled by the abilities with which we have been gifted. In Psalm 34, we find the following:

> Who desires life, loving each day to see good?
> Then guard your tongue from evil and your lips from speaking deceit.
> Turn from evil and do good; seek peace and pursue it.

It's a tall order and gives us much to contemplate in the upcoming period of introspection, reflection, and repentance. However, there is one element in the psalm on which I would like to focus. The first area that we are told to work on is our speech. In this pandemic, when the one part of the body that we are obligated to cover is our mouths, it would be difficult to avoid hearing the clear and powerful message, i.e., that we must improve our speech.

Especially in this pandemic, when other forms of social interaction are being limited, we are being left with many, many words. In Zoom meetings, videos, memes, e-mails etc. much is being written, said, read, and forwarded. But we have *always* been "the creature that speaks." And we do much good, but also much harm, with our words. Hurtful speech, slanderous gossip, cutting remarks, undermining sarcasm, hateful criticism, all poison our world at least as much as the coronavirus. And with a much longer history. With, in all probability, more lasting effects.

One of the reasons for the shofar, which I heard recently, is that its sounds constitute a form of prayer. Unfortunately, our mouths have become blemished through the improper speech which has issued from them. So we employ a shofar, which has the same letters in Hebrew as the word "*shahper*," meaning "to improve."

And without potentially harmful words, but with a wordless sound that emanates from our very souls, we beseech Hashem to forgive us for our problematic speech in the past and to please vouchsafe us a good year with myriads of blessings of health, parnassa, and peace. In return, we resolve to improve our words, our deeds and our relationships. Because We Choose Life!

Shana Tova!

September 25, 2020

Coronese Mathematics

(With apologies to my husband, the mathematician.)

6,700. What an awful number! I began my day hearing the announcement that it represented the number of new coronavirus cases in 24 hours here in the Holyland on Planet Corona. And I just heard another horrific number. 59. The number of corona deaths in one day. Today. I'm beginning to hate Coronese math.

I have to be careful with that last statement. In 1992, Mattel introduced a talking Barbie doll. One of "her" recorded statements was, "Math class is tough." This brought down upon their heads the wrath of feminists. It was deemed highly prejudicial and anti-women to suggest that they might not excel in mathematics. Naturally, Mattel apologized profusely and withdrew the doll from the shelves. Naturally.

Still, while I had little trouble with "math class" in my school years, I am having a very difficult time with the numerical tyranny here on Planet Corona. As of now, we can venture 1,000 meters (we thought it was to be only 500) from our front door. Of course, we must maintain 2 meters of social distance from others. Which is 6 feet (approximately) for the non-metric amongst us. Then there are 14 days of quarantine if you've been exposed to someone who's tested positive or if you've just returned from abroad. However, sometimes it's really only 10 days and there are situations when it's five days (just don't ask me what they are!).

Each day, on the front page of the Times of Israel, there is a prominent table with all the terrible statistics of the pandemic. Today's are Cases: 209,635; Recovered: 148,417; Serious cases: 685; Deaths: 1,376. Then you have the global statistics. Global cases: 32,306,913; Deaths 985,224.

Now, don't you feel better for having all these numbers at your fingertips? No? How surprising! To be honest, I never pay attention to this feature of the TOI. I rarely look at the newspapers at all. But I am finding the numbers of the pandemic to be very disturbing, depersonalizing, and ultimately, numbing.

As the High Holidays approached, the government established several criteria for determining how many congregants could pray inside a synagogue. It depended on area, number of entrances and exits, windows, and several other numerical particulars.

It was so complicated that some wag produced a fake help-wanted ad for a gabbai for a synagogue in Ness Tziona. The requirements were that he must have an advanced degree in mathematics and preferably another in engineering. Oh, and a working knowledge of synagogue ritual and prayer would be helpful. The Great Synagogue in Jerusalem decided that the rules were so complex that they would prefer not to open. Besides, who knew when the criteria might be altered.

Arguably, numbers conceal more than they reveal. They can even deaden our sensitivity. To know that 6,000,000 Jews died during the Holocaust can have the effect of almost trivializing the immensity of the horror. It's a number that we can't imagine and which, thereby, is powerless to convey the extent of our losses.

The Nazis tattooed numbers on victims to deprive them of any individual value in the interests of efficiency! Those numbers hid the infinite worth of a single life. Whereas the diary of a single and singular young woman named Anne Frank brought home the tragedy of the destruction of European Jewry more powerfully.

Jewish tradition has a complex relationship with mathematical concepts and language. Jewish law is replete with numbers and measures of all kinds. One of the Five Books of the Torah is entitled, although not by Jews, the Book of Numbers. This reflects the fact that it contains two instances of a census of the People of Israel, one at the beginning and one at the end of the book.

Nevertheless, outside of a prescribed census, counting the Jewish people, or even groups of Jews, is forbidden. When King David orders a census of his people, it results in a national disaster. Our Sages tell us that blessing only devolves on that which is uncounted and unmeasured.

However, there is one number that has great power and significance. The number "one." Each day, the Jew declares the Unity of God in the centerpiece of prayer, the Shema. We are a unique and singular nation. When the Torah describes the encampment of Am Yisrael, the People of Israel, at Mount Sinai, it uses the singular form of the verb "to camp" causing Rashi to comment that we received the Torah as "One man with one heart," signifying a unity that we have rarely managed to replicate either before or after.

We are on the eve of Yom Kippur, otherwise known as the Day of Atonement, or At-*one*-ment, when we once again unite with Hashem having cleansed ourselves of our sins in a process of Teshuva, Return.

In one of the central prayers of the Yom Kippur liturgy, the *U'Netaneh Tokef,* the liturgical poet presents a metaphorical image of God as shepherd, causing His flock to pass, one by one, before Him and marking each with his fate for the coming year. Each individual member receiving individual attention. One at a time.

Additionally, in the Musaf afternoon prayer of Yom Kippur, there is a vivid and detailed description of the unique Temple service performed by the High Priest on this day. One of the essential rituals is the sprinkling of blood before the Holy of Holies. And we recite the counting of the High Priest as he enumerates the sprinklings. One, one and one, one and two, etc. One. Always one. It appears to be a central element of this unique day.

Perhaps the antidote to the depersonalizing and numbing effect of Corona numbers is to focus on the number "one." We can relate personally to each person with whom we come into contact. We can try to take our challenges one day at a time. We can remember that personal growth and improved coping techniques can only be achieved by taking one step after another, and not attempting to leap ahead too quickly. That often results in failure and disillusion.

And perhaps most importantly, we can strive to improve our relationship with The One, especially in these Days of Awe on Planet Corona.

Shema Yisrael, Hashem Elokeinu, Hashem Echad!

Listen, O Israel, the Lord is our God, the Lord is One!

September 27, 2020

A Coronation on Planet Corona and the Power of '*Atah*'

The trumpets blared! (Although they were actually shofars.) And we were all present at a Coronation. Not as bystanding observers, but as active participants. Indeed, *we* were the ones to place the crown upon the head of the King. And, although it did not transpire in a beautiful and lofty edifice, but rather in a Jerusalem parking lot, it was nonetheless an awe-inspiring moment.

Those who have viewed the Netflix series *The Crown* have some sense of the pomp and ceremony connected with a coronation, having witnessed the elaborate ceremony as Elizabeth Windsor became Queen Elizabeth II of England 67 years ago.

There are some who recall seeing the event live at the time or via television, as Elizabeth's coronation was the first to be televised in full by the BBC and also the first major world event to be broadcast internationally on television. And all that for a queen whose powers, activities, and influence are largely ceremonial!

Not so, the coronation of the King of Kings! Though we have been designated to proclaim his Kingship and although, on some level, "there is no King without a Nation," still Hashem's power is absolute, over all creation and all of history. And on Planet Corona, the Corona-tion of Hashem is a particularly awesome and momentous event. Hashem's infinite power and control of events have become unquestionably vivid.

The proclamation of the rise of a new monarch is usually preceded, at least so we've read, by the words, "The king is dead, long live the king!" Of course, that could not apply to what happens on Rosh Hashana or to our relationship to Hashem's Kingship. Or perhaps it could. This year in particular.

In his book *Seeing God*, Rabbi David Aaron writes that he was never perturbed by Nietzsche's proclamation that "God is dead." Because he largely agrees. He writes that a colleague's standard response to an atheist is, "The God you don't believe in, I don't believe in either."

The perpetrator of the Big Bang who set everything in motion and then went into retirement? *He* is dead. The deity that is somewhere "up there" and doesn't interfere with the world? *He* is dead. And the deity that can be bought off by gifts and sacrifices? *He* doesn't exist, as our prophets repeatedly warn us. Especially, the deity that some of us believe we need to defend with vehemence and "baseless hatred" against others of His children who don't agree with us? *He* doesn't exist, either.

But neither does the image, prominent in the last few decades, of a warm and fuzzy, kindly, and bearded Old Man, the "kumbaya" Lord who loves us unconditionally and wants us to be happy, comfortable, and warm. And makes few difficult demands. Who loves you "just the way you are."

Anyone who has been following the Torah readings of the last few weeks in the Book of Devarim is aware of the dire warnings and predictions of the measures that Hashem will take if we do not follow His commands.

Furthermore, Jewish history shows that very difficult and even horrific events *have indeed* befallen us, often mirroring the predictions in the Torah. In those passages, the presented image is of a Deity who is exacting and Who doesn't overlook our wrongful actions.

Maimonides writes in *The Guide to the Perplexed* that when large-scale national calamity befalls us, we are *absolutely obligated* to punctiliously examine our deeds and return in repentance. Otherwise, we are considered "cruel." As long as the deeds that we see as needing correction are our own and not someone else's.

Don't misunderstand. Of course, the Hashem that we *should* and *must* believe in and whose Existence is beyond our understanding *does* indeed love us. No less this year than any other. But *this* year we understand that Hashem's approach must sometimes be one of "tough love." And, at times, that is the only form of real love that is healthy and appropriate for His creations.

It may even be true that He is saying at this moment, "This hurts Me more than it hurts you." As it says in the Talmud (Brachot 3a), a mournful voice emanates from Heaven daily, saying "Woe to the Father who has banished His children from His table, and woe to the children who have been banished from His table."

For, of course, Hashem is also our Father. Our loving Father. Our King, but our Father, too. This nexus of two of Hashem's unlimited titles happens on Yom Kippur. One of the centerpieces of the Yom Kippur liturgy is the enactment of the Temple service performed by the High Priest. One of the most moving and powerful elements occurs when the prayer leader chants:

> And the priests and all the people who were standing in the courtyard, when they heard the glorious and awesome name spoken out expressly by the High Priest in holiness and purity, would bend their knees and bow down and give thanks and fall upon their faces and say: "Blessed be the name of His glorious kingdom forever and all time."

At this point, in many prayer gatherings, all the congregants actually kneel, prostrate themselves, and bring their faces to the floor to reenact this sublime act of total submission to the Will of God. Three times during the service. Only on Yom Kippur.

I find this act supremely moving and even exhilarating. Perhaps because it is such a rare gesture, it is so much more powerful. This year, in particular, I need to show myself that there is no alternative to total submission to Hashem's Will. Who or what else is in charge? Any ideas?

And then we come to what is perhaps the most poignant and even heart-rending prayer of this season, *Avina Malkeinu*, "Our Father, our King," in which we petition Hashem to send us blessings and remove all the difficulties which have been sent our way and are still plaguing us. We petition that He do this in the merit of the martyrs throughout history.

At the end we ask our Father and King: "Be gracious to us and answer us, though we have no worthy deeds; act with us in charity and loving-kindness and save us." And each line is prefaced with the address, "Our Father, our King." Father, first. Then, King.

We've been granted a special relationship with Hashem. He permits us to call him "Father." He even sets aside His honor and allows us to address his Paternal relationship to us *before* His powerful Kingship and dominion over us. Further, in many of our prayers, in fact in every one of our blessings, we employ the second person singular, the word "Atah," in addressing Him. This might even be considered an overly familiar form of address.

Teachers, sages, and even parents are sometimes addressed in the third person to maintain the distance necessary to ward off familiarity which can breed... well, you know. Nonetheless, Hashem not only permits it, but encourages and even legislates it.

Perhaps, one of the problems is that, in modern English, there is no counterpart to the alternate second-person address once employed, i.e., the words "thou" and "thee." The form that still exists in modern French as in "Je t'aime." That form suggests intimacy rather than problematic familiarity.

It is represented in the word "Atah" as we use it to address Hashem. Because there is such a danger in feeling that Hashem is distant from us, unapproachable, perhaps even uncaring, Hashem, as it were, goes to extraordinary lengths to assure us that He is here. Now. Attentive. Caring.

That is the combined power of Hashem as King and Parent. Or, rather, as Parent and King. We are obligated to submit and accept His Will, and, particularly this year, have no other alternative. At the same time, however, we realize that Hashem is our loving, but exacting Parent who, for all the best reasons, and for our benefit, must do, not always what we like, but rather what we need.

An exquisite Midrash found in the Talmud (Brachot 7a) tells of an incident that occurred in the Temple on Yom Kippur:

> It was taught; Rabbi Yishmael the son of Elisha said: "I once entered into the innermost [part of the sanctuary], to offer incense, and I saw Akatrie-l K-ah (a name referring to the crown of God), the Lord of Hosts, seated upon a high and exalted throne. He said to me, 'Yishmael my son, bless Me!' I said, 'May it be Your will that Your mercy suppresses Your anger, and that Your mercy prevail over Your other attributes, and that You deal with Your children with the attribute of mercy, and that You deal with them beyond the letter of the law.' And He nodded to me with His head and accepted the blessing.

Blessed art *Thou*, O Lord our God (and Father), and may it be so!

September 30, 2020

Gulliver Travels to Planet Corona

In 1726, author and satirist Jonathan Swift wrote *Gulliver's Travels*, the tale of Lemuel Gulliver, ship's surgeon, who travels the world discovering strange places, people, and customs. The book was instantly popular and is still considered a satiric masterpiece of thinly veiled and largely misanthropic commentary on early 18th-century politics, events, women, governments, and in general, on the human race.

Two of the best-remembered countries he visits are Lilliput, home to tiny humans, and Brobdingnag, home of giants. I recall reading the book when I was a child. The satire and parody were largely lost on me, but the images of the very small and exceedingly large humans have remained vivid.

I was thinking of *Gulliver's Travels* as I myself have been exploring Planet Corona. Particularly during and after Yom Kippur this year, the images of Lilliputians and Brobdingnagians entered my thoughts as I contemplated the inhabitants of this planet. (Incidentally, both "lilliputian" and brobdingnagian" have entered the English lexicon as adjectives for "very tiny" and for "enormous.")

These thoughts were particularly apt for Yom Kippur this year for, as I learned in one of the many pre-Yom Kippur talks I listened to, this is the one day of the year when we get to view humans, particularly ourselves, from Hashem's perspective.

As we read the listing of human failings for which we need to repent, we find, by contrast, the qualities that Hashem wishes for us. Our personal stature, consequently, depends on adopting and practicing the desirable qualities laid out in the day's prayers.

However, unlike in *Gullliver's Travels,* the inhabitants of Planet Corona, or the Coronese, are *both* lilliputian and brobdingnagian. And the appropriate adjective applies, not to their physical size, but to their ethical, spiritual, and humane stature. So, we have "little people" here, whose personal world is petty and small and contains sympathy mainly for themselves, *their* concerns, *their* agendas, *their* communities, even *their* political bedfellows.

Many believe themselves to be very important, worthy of respect, and very significant in their own estimation. But, in reality, they are narrow, limited, sectarian, and even threaten the general well-being. They often strive to enlarge themselves by diminishing others, usually through negative and even hateful speech.

Their "littleness" was described by Eleanor Roosevelt, who famously quipped, "Great minds discuss ideas; average minds discuss events; small minds discuss people." And, unfortunately, these are often the ones who grab the headlines and appear in the media. For the Lilliputians sell newspapers and attract media attention. Unfortunately.

However, we also have brobdingnagian giants of the spirit among us. They are the ones with large and generous souls. Those who encompass others, including those unlike them, in their compassion and concern. Great people who are often modest as to their own needs, yet desirous of helping others. You have to look for them, however, as they generally go quietly about their good works, shy away from the limelight, and are rarely interesting to the media.

Sometimes, these giants are motivated by the desire to make the world a better place, even a little bit better, through their efforts. To leave behind a good name. That was the motivation for Albert Nobel who established the prestigious Nobel Prize. His "awakening" took place in the following way:

> When Alfred's brother Ludwig died in 1888, a French newspaper mistakenly published Alfred's obituary. Reading his own obituary Nobel was disgusted to find out his public image. The newspaper condemned Nobel for inventing dynamite, giving him the infamous nickname *Le marchand de la mort est mort* ("The merchant of death is dead") and went on to say *"Dr. Alfred Nobel, who became rich by finding ways to kill more people faster than ever before, died yesterday."*
>
> To Alfred, this obituary was a warning. He spent his lifetime alone inventing things and was deeply disturbed and concerned with how he would be remembered. This unfortunate event inspired him to make alterations in his will, to improve his public image, and to be remembered for a good cause. (From *The Vintage News*)

But, here on our planet, we have perhaps greater giants. These are exceptional people, who never saw themselves as such, who were catalyzed to greatness by tragedy. When Rabbi Seth and Sherri Mandel's son Koby was viciously killed by Palestinian terrorists in May 2001, they turned their horrific experience into the Koby Mandel Foundation which does so much for the families of terrorist victims.

Similarly, the family of Malki Roth, a 15-year-old killed in the infamous Sbarro terrorist homicide attack in August 2001, founded Keren Malki, an organization that supports families of children with disabilities. These are people who were able to snatch victories of the human spirit from the jaws of defeat and despair.

A young couple we know well, Devorah and Evan Schendler, made aliya to Ramat Beit Shemesh a few years ago. Last year, in the month of Av, a baby was born to them. Shortly after the birth, the parents were informed that their newborn had a rare syndrome which was, as the doctors put it, "incompatible with living."

They knew then that their child would have a very short sojourn on the planet. Yet they somehow found within themselves, their four other children, and loving friends and family, the needed resources to cope with their shock and grief. They were determined to love and cherish their child, Netanel Yakir, for as long as was given them to do so.

Fifty-one days after his birth, between Rosh Hashana and Yom Kippur of last year, Hashem brought Netanel Yakir home. The funeral was packed with weeping friends and family, but we all drew strength from the dignity and courage of the parents. Devorah spoke magnificently, with great faith and honesty.

During the course of the following year, this crazy year, the family strove to find ways to derive and share deeper meaning from the precious but brief life of their child.

A few weeks ago, they opened a 51-day initiative in Netanel Yakir's memory. Mirroring the span of his life are the 51 days from Rosh Chodesh Elul until Hoshana Raba, which is the annual period in the Jewish calendar of soul-searching, repentance, and self-improvement.

They introduced the program urging people to adopt some action, no matter how seemingly minor, towards improving an imperfect characteristic or behavior. Simultaneously, Devorah undertook to send daily e-mails to all those who participated in this initiative, with inspirational quotes, stories, and short essays.

A year ago, when their baby passed away the Schendlers imagined that at his yahrtzeit there would be an appropriate memorial program of some kind. However, as the pandemic made that impossible, they instead made a beautiful, touching, and inspirational film about their experiences and about the project.

The film includes messages from some of the many participants in the initiative, attesting to the myriad of personal improvement undertakings that have enhanced their lives and the lives of others. What an amazing testament to the memory of Netanel Yakir and his "giant" parents, even if their stature will be recognized best elsewhere and at another time.

I doubt if any one of us desires to face tragedy in order to grow. However, we can take a page from the book of Alfred Nobel and imagine what we will be remembered for. Not what our own obituary will look like. They are most often air-brushed, to say the least. But what will be written in the Book of Life in which we signed our names during the Days of Awe. Yes, signed our names.

Many of us think, erroneously, that our names are entered in Hashem's Book. But the actual translation is "and every man's signature appears there." We sign up for the type of year we hope to have and the type of person we hope to become. It's up to us to aim for a year of either greatness or pettiness.

I believe that the place to begin is with our speech. So much good and so much harm emerges from the mouth. Not only droplets of virus can wreak havoc on the world. So can words. If we refrain from speaking or writing with anger, hatred, malice, and shaming, it's so much less likely that we will act in these negative ways. As Eleanor Roosevelt suggests, best not to talk about other people at all.

One of the laws of sukka is that it is wrong to bring into the sukka inappropriate items such as cooking pots, utensils, and trash collectors. The Chafetz Chaim in his Mishna Berura notes that if inappropriate items must not enter the sukka, how much more so inappropriate speech.

For that reason, we have created place-cards for our guests that welcome them to our sukka and quote this law from the Mishna Berura. Our speech is an excellent place to begin our growth.

It's our choice. So many of our options have been severely limited this year. But one has been vouchsafed to us and cannot be denied. The option to be bigger than we have been, better than before, bountiful in our love and in our deeds.

Lilliputian or Brobdingnagian? Sign up for your choice.

Chapter Eight

October 2020

October 2, 2020

And You Will Be Exceedingly Joyful

I love Sukkot. I always have. Growing up in New England, we were among the very few families that had personal sukkot (booths). In fact, my Jewish day school held classes during Chol Hamoed Sukkot in order to give students the opportunity to eat in a sukka. We didn't mind having school. I had not yet heard of Sukkot trips or tiyulim. And Great Adventure didn't yet exist.

Each year, my father built a small wooden sukka and covered it over with freshly cut pine. Yes, we had pine needles in our soup but, once again, I didn't know there was an alternative. The first time I saw bamboo *schach* (when I visited family in New York), I was aghast. That's not schach! Even after I married and lived in New York, we managed to arrange for pine schach. I loved the smell.

We beautified the sukka with homemade decorations. We made birds with eggshell bodies. My mother, a"h, showed us how to pierce the eggs and blow out the contents. We hung *real* fruit and made paper chains. Our largest decoration, and the one that lasted from year to year, was a framed picture of the Gaon of Vilna.

Sometimes, being in New England, we sat and ate in the sukka with jackets and scarves. but we never thought to do otherwise. Indeed, my most vociferous female equality outburst took place on a Sukkot when I was a teen. My parents had invited a family for a meal but, as our sukka was really only large enough for our immediate family, it meant that the females would eat indoors. I had a fit.

At the time, I was much less aware of the different obligations of men and women in Jewish law. I felt absolutely discriminated against. I've since gotten over it. Nevertheless, because I so love Sukkot I very rarely eat anything at all outside of the sukka.

Which brings us to Sukkot on Planet Corona. As we approached the first of the *Shalosh Regalim,* the Three-Festival Cycle that begins with Pesach, moves on to Shavuot, and ends with Sukkot, we never would have imagined that we would still be on Planet Corona for the upcoming holiday. But we are. And not only that, we are actually *commanded* to be *b'simcha*, joyful, on this holiday.

In fact, when the Gaon of Vilna was asked by his students what, in his opinion, was the most difficult commandment to perform, they were surprised that he singled out the command to be joyful on the holidays, and particularly on Sukkot! The reason being that we must not only rejoice when we *feel* like doing so, but also, and especially, when we *don't*! Because it's a commandment and doesn't depend on our mood or circumstances.

But perhaps that's too great a demand for this year on Planet Corona. For many of us, much of the joy of the chag is in family gatherings, having guests at our table, and in participating in the many Chol Hamoed activities planned for this time of year. To say nothing of the nightly celebrations of Simchat Beit Hashoeva,* particularly all around the city of Jerusalem.

And then there is Simchat Torah! We so look forward to the joyful celebrations as we complete our yearly cycle of readings from the Torah and begin a new cycle immediately. This year, we worry and mourn. What will be? What kind of Sukkot can we celebrate in the midst of this pandemic? How will our children remember this year's "joyous" holiday?

Yet, we are *obligated* to be in "simcha." So, we need to change our outlook, even if we can't change our circumstances. We need to revisit our celebrations, our customs and… our sukka. In the tractate of Sukkah (11b), Rabbi Eliezer and Rabbi Akiva disagree as to the nature of the "sukka" in which we are commanded to dwell for the seven days of Sukkot.

Rabbi Eliezer maintains that it is to remind us of the *Ananei Hakavod* (Clouds of Glory) which surrounded and protected the Jewish People for all the years that they dwelled in the desert. Rabbi Akiva says that our sukkot are to remind us of the *actual* impermanent, unadorned, and portable domiciles that we lived in for 40 years.

Why be reminded that we once lived in simple "shacks?" And why replicate that today? Our Sages say that it is to remind us of the fragility and impermanence of our existence. In our spacious, congenial, and sturdy homes we feel protected from the elements, secure, comfortable, established, even, perhaps, a bit "immortal."

Our homes also afford us an opportunity to enjoy and, perhaps, proclaim our ever-increasing material "worth." In Jewish neighborhoods everywhere, building and expansion of luxurious homes proceeds apace. Large homes and apartments are being enlarged, far beyond what has ever before existed. "Edifice complex," indeed.

So, on Sukkot we are commanded to move outside of these "gods of wood and stone" and live in more modest domiciles. To remind us that, even in our sturdy homes, we are, in reality, vulnerable, fragile, unprotected from the vicissitudes of illness, war, extreme weather, and all the usual and unusual threats that are always with us. We are cautioned that the terra firma beneath our feet, or the marble flooring, can collapse at any time.

Well, do we really need to be reminded of all that *this year?* I venture to suggest that our move to Planet Corona has made all that abundantly clear. I can remain in *my home* and experience my vulnerability and fragility. I don't need the help of the sukka, thank you very much!

But let us not forget the opinion of Rabbi Eliezer, that our sukka reminds us of the *Ananei Ha'kavod.* What were these "Clouds of Glory?" They were Hashem's way of protecting and embracing us from the moment we left Egypt. The Midrash says that they surrounded and sheltered us from snakes and scorpions, from desert storms, and from foreign enemies. They reminded us that Hashem was always with us and, although we were in a howling wilderness, *Lo ira rah, ki atah imahdi* "I will fear no evil, for Thou art with me" (Psalm 23). These clouds represented, for the newly released nation, a loving and protecting Presence.

However, the Midrash continues, when the nation sinned with the Golden Calf, Hashem withdrew those clouds, leaving us vulnerable to outside threats and to His own anger. Only after a period of pleading, punishment, and penitence were the *Ananei Hakavod* returned. This occurred when the Israelites began building the Tabernacle, the place where Hashem would "dwell in your midst." The date? The 15th of Tishrei. The day the holiday of Sukkot begins.

Our Sages tell us that there are only three commandments that we enter into with our entire bodies, which envelope us, and into which we immerse ourselves. They are the mitzvot of mikva, sukka, and living in Israel.

On Yom Kippur, Rabbi Akiva tells us, Hashem is referred to as *Mikva Yisrael*, the One who cleanses us so that we can be reborn and renewed after the process of repentance. So, we have been reborn.

Then, we enter into the sukka. The A"ri suggests that the symbolism of the two and a half walls necessary for a sukka to be considered kosher is that of a hug, if you can envision two of the walls being your arm above and below your elbow and the half wall being your hand. We have been reborn, and now, we are being cradled and embraced.

And who couldn't use a hug right about now? The fact that I, along with many others, am also privileged to be able to experience all this in Israel makes it a glorious trifecta!

So, let us be joyous this Sukkot. We can luxuriate in our dependence on a Power much greater than any that we have previously trusted. Let us be reminded of the wonderful Nation to which we belong with an open acceptance we once had before we "learned" who we should like and who we shouldn't.

We should absorb the lesson of the *Arba Minim*, the Four Species, which, according to one explanation, each symbolize a different type of Jew and yet must be held together in order to properly fulfill the commandment.

Let's be children. Small children are generally made happy by small things. They have no need of expensive toys, programs, and devices (unless they have been terribly spoiled at a very young age.) I have one set of grandchildren that I always say are very easily pleased. I playfully add that if you gave one of them a rubber band, their reaction would be, "Wow! A rubber band! That is so amazing! Thank you sooo much!"

We, too, can make ourselves happy, even joyous. But it won't just happen.

The Gemara gives guidelines on pleasing various members of a household. For the grown men, joy comes from meat and wine, for women, with jewelry and new clothing, for children, with treats and sweets. This year, there was no reason for me to purchase new clothing or jewelry. I have plenty as it is. But, as a "child," I have put in a supply of chocolate, sweet wine, and Ben and Jerry's ice cream. I also have placed my new hammock in the sukka.

Some will have to make do with less. Some with more. But we can choose to bask in Hashem's protective embrace. And we can hug back by being "*ach samech*," "exceedingly joyful."

Chag Sameach!

---

* The Rejoicing of the Water-Drawing. A special celebration held during the Intermediate days of Sukkot.

October 11, 2020

A Final Trip to the Ministry

I've been summoned to the Ministry. I received notice of an appointment at the Department of Information and Communication. Only this time, no one else seems to have gotten such an "invitation." Just me. And so, I wonder what's going on? What have I done?

Due to the present lockdown, I have remained close to home (or to sukka, as it happens). Therefore, this is the farthest I've ventured in quite a while. As I approach the center of town and the ministry building, I notice a flurry of unexpected and unusual activity.

Workers are rushing around wearing protective clothing and carrying *cans of paint*! What is all *that* about? Is there some city renewal project of which I haven't been informed? The scene reminds me of something, but I can't quite remember what it is. The association is nibbling at the corner of my memory, but won't come forward.

After I enter the ministry building and have my temperature checked, I am directly ushered into the office of Mar* Benny Bilbul,** the deputy Minister of Communications. Now, I am really nervous!

He invites me to take a chair and seats himself behind a large desk covered with newspapers, documents and, of course, the latest model laptop. I notice that he looks rather nervous and seems not to know how to begin. He clears his throat several times and then finds his voice.

"Good morning, Geveret*** Passow. I understand that you have been writing a series that you have entitled 'Letters from Planet Corona.' Is that correct?"

I'm not sure whether to be flattered or not. I am certainly confused. However, I answer in the affirmative.

"Well," he expostulates, "you have to stop!"

Now I am *really* confused. "But why?" I ask. "I haven't written anything problematic, have I? What could you possibly object to?"

I don't bother asking how he *knows* about my e-mails or about what they contain. I know better.

"It's not what you write," he continues. "It's the address. You can't be sending letters from Planet Corona, as there is no such place. We are not on it and we never have been!"

"Are you saying there is no coronavirus pandemic?" I ask in astonishment.

I am also a bit frightened. Are government officials now taking their place among the conspiracy theorists? The ones who deny the existence of a pandemic, suggesting all sorts of insane theories about why the world's governments are deluding and frightening us?

"No, no," Mar Bilbul assures me, "*of course* there is a pandemic. A serious one. And we must take all proper precautions. In fact," he continues as an aside," we are pleased that in your letters you encourage proper wearing of masks and social distancing. No, we only object to the fact that you are promulgating the idea that the world's population has somehow taken up residence on a non-existent planet."

"What on *earth* are you talking about?" I ask in exasperation.

"Exactly right," he responds. "That's where we are. Earth. Always have been. Never left."

"But we've been persuaded, by you as a matter of fact, that we are on a new planet called Corona and have been for some time. And now you're saying that it's *not true*? How did this come about?" I am desperately trying to make some sense of these revelations.

"Geveret Passow, I will tell you something in confidence. Although it will probably come out sooner or later. The whole thing has been a 'prank' perpetrated by a couple of astrophysics graduate students at Stanford University who were in quarantine with Covid-19 in the early months of the pandemic.

"They collaborated with two talented hackers, also in quarantine, at the Haifa Technion to devise a hoax with the same global dimensions as the pandemic. It appears that they were successful. In fact, all the venture capital people in Silicon Valley are at the moment pursuing them aggressively waving checkbooks at them. It's even possible that Zoom financed the hoax entirely."

"But how did they do it? How did they perpetrate such a vast hoax?" I ask disbelievingly. It seems impossible to me.

"They did it with *highly advanced algorithms*," Mar Bilbul says in a hushed voice with a touch of awe.

"Ah," I say slowly. "Algorithms. Now, I understand." Well, not really. I simply know that "algorithm" is the magic word behind all the good and all the evil of modern technology. (I have just watched the Big Tech exposé *The Social Dilemma*. Very sobering.)

I assure Mar Bilbul that I will no longer be sending my letters from Planet Corona and he seems very relieved. I then recall all the painters running around outside and ask him if he knows anything about it.

He answers, "We are painting over the signs that use the word "Corona" which we put up after we were fooled into believing that we had moved to a new planet. I admit we may have gone slightly overboard. You are free to take some samples of Terra Beer on your way out. And thank you for being so understanding. You realize, I hope, that this is most embarrassing for us."

I offer him my sympathy and take my leave. As I exit the building, I realize that I am still somewhat in shock. This has been a thoroughly unexpected revelation. What am I to make of all of this? What of all the letters I've written as if we were on a totally foreign planet? It will take some time and much thought to assimilate and make some sense of what I've just learned.

In the meantime, I recall what it is that the workers running around with paint cans reminded me of. A memorable incident in *Alice in Wonderland*, when Alice wanders into the garden of the hot-headed Queen of Hearts and sees the gardeners (who are actually playing cards) frantically painting the white rose bushes red.

They explain, in their panic, that the queen had ordered that red rose bushes be planted and they had, accidentally, planted white roses instead. They are trying to correct the error before the queen visits the garden and peremptorily orders "Off with their heads!" (the gardeners' heads, not the flowers').

I am going home to think. How do I understand my visit to the Ministry and how will I explain it all to my friends and readers?

I do have one post-Sukkot thought. It actually relates to the Days of Repentance. How fortunate for us that we have been vouchsafed a process whereby our "red" sins, once represented by a red string tied to the horn of the "scapegoat," can be transformed into a pure white string, signaling that we have been cleansed of our sins. A process that "saves our heads." A gift from Our King. Whatever planet we happen to be on!

* Mr.
** Play on words. Hebrew for "confusion."
*** Mrs.

October 14, 2020

Planet Corona, Then and Now

Have you ever had the following experience? You are reading something and, inexplicably, a common word that you have seen countless times appears to be spelled incorrectly. Or, alternatively, you are writing and can't recall how to spell an everyday word that would have appeared on your second-grade spelling test. (Do they still have those, I wonder?)

It appears to be a very common phenomenon and, unsurprisingly, there is a name for it. Wordnesia. However, what *is* surprising is that no one seems to know why it occurs.

Kyle Mahowald, a PhD candidate in linguistics at MIT, says it appears to happen when you over-focus on a word. It's generally temporary and it seems to be a product of the fact that much of our reading is done on automatic pilot.

You have probably been intrigued by those passages in which the words have all but the first and last letters in a garbled order. Most people find that they can read them surprisingly fluently.

Yet, you could be reading a passage of normally written words and experience that "glitch" where a common word looks misspelled. That's because, for some reason, you are now focusing on the letters more than on the words. On the trees rather than on the forest. Wordnesia.

However, it's not only reading that is usually, and often usefully, done on automatic pilot. Humans are also creatures of "habitual perception." According to the Center for the Transformation of Habitual Perception,

> Life requires that we put on blinkers; we must not look to the right, to the left, or behind, but straight ahead, in the direction in which we are supposed to walk. In order to live, we must be selective in our knowledge and our memories, and retain only that which may contribute to our action upon things.

It goes on to say that while this is a useful tool for getting things done *efficiently* in our world, it doesn't leave much room for reflection or contemplation:

> Human beings have focused so much on becoming experts on their "actions upon things" and, to speak generally, so little on their reflective capacities, that we have become a global civilization of consumers.

Basically, this means that, once again, we do so much on "automatic pilot" that we hardly notice or reflect upon much that exists and happens in our world.

According to Wikipedia, "defamiliarization" is a technique of presenting things in an *unfamiliar or strange* way so that your audience can "gain new perspectives and see the world differently... it is the central concept of art and poetry." By defamiliarizing, we are taken off "automatic pilot" and given an opportunity to see and experience differently.

And all of the above is by way of explaining "how and why" we have been together on Planet Corona. Approximately eight months ago, we entered perhaps the most gargantuan, high-impact, world-wide, mind-boggling example of *radical defamiliarization* imaginable.

The comfortable, largely predictable planet that most of us were familiar with was rendered totally alien in every possible way we could conceive. And even to those for whom the planet had always been less hospitable, the additional strains, fears, and attendant hardships of the pandemic made life even more threatening and difficult.

And, so, we "landed" on Planet Corona. There was some comfort in imagining that we were no longer on the home planet we had known all our lives, but rather on a foreign planet where all the elements of the pandemic were interesting, but less threatening, aspects of an *"unfamiliar and strange"* new world where we proceeded to *"gain new perspectives and see the world differently."* Our world had been defamiliarized.

However, rather than deal with a Planet Earth that was frighteningly transformed or with the radical changes in our human lives on our home turf, it was easier to attribute *all that* to a new and far-off place that, most importantly, we might one day be able to leave behind us, along with all its unpleasant aspects.

There was a strong element in this of emotional and psychological "dissociation" which occurs when people undergo traumatic experiences over which they have no control. But this dissociation, this imagined Planet Corona, also contained a more benign and very positive feature. It allowed for a somewhat more detached and even objective perspective on the last eight months.

We could look at this "place" we were in and see some of the humor, quirks, anomalies, and even positive elements of our situation. We were catapulted out of "habitual perception" and, essentially, *forced* to view the familiar in unfamiliar ways. To reflect on what we had heretofore taken for granted. Things such as family, health, economic stability, even religious values and practices.

219

And being on a foreign planet was also humbling. You don't expect to know everything when you are in a foreign *country*, let alone a foreign *planet*. Bill Bryson, writing on being an expatriate, puts it this way:

> I can't think of anything that excites a greater sense of childlike wonder than to be in a country where you are ignorant of almost everything. Suddenly you are five years old again. You can't read anything, you have only the most rudimentary sense of how things work, you can't even reliably cross a street without endangering your life. Your whole existence becomes a series of interesting guesses.

What we have all been experiencing is not a case of "*word*nesia" but rather "*world*nesia!"

However, ultimately, we all *know* we've never really left home. Another world traveler, Terry Pratchett wrote:

> Why do you go away? So that you can come back. So that you can see the place you came from with new eyes and extra colors. And the people there see you differently, too. Coming back to where you started is not the same as never leaving.

So, we realize that we haven't *really* traveled far at all. Certainly not to another planet. Still, we may be viewing our home with "new eyes and extra colors." It's likely that we are also seeing each other differently. By "leaving," if only in imagination, we still have the advantage of "returning" to our home base with all the wisdom, experiences, and "souvenirs" we've acquired during our voyage.

So, what *have* we picked up? Certainly, many of us have a far greater appreciation for the taken-for-granted blessings we were used to and which have been affected. We now miss, and therefore value, many aspects of our pre-pandemic lives.

We yearn for our simple familial and friendly interactions such as visits, get-togethers, family meals, and guests at our tables. And, of course, the hugs. We now long for the return of comforting and pleasant routines such as attending classes, exercising in gyms, going to work, praying in shul, even routine medical and dental visits.

When we read of Covid-19 victims, we remember to be grateful for our health. When we hear of those who perished due to the virus, we fervently give thanks for life. Reading of people on respirators reminds us of how appreciative we ought to be for every breath we take.

One of the deepest and, hopefully lasting, lessons from this pandemic is that *we are not in charge!* Not at all. We've seen our fate, the world's fate, wrenched from our hands. However, we now know that it never really *was* in our hands. We can still influence our personal lives in important and useful ways. But the communal, national, and global issues are beyond us. Beyond all of us.

It can be hoped that this has led us to greater humility. We thought that with advances in health care, unprecedented economic prosperity, global cooperation, scientific advances, and exponential growth in technology and AI, we could face *any* challenge. We could answer any questions that could be posed. But we were wrong. In a million cases, dead wrong!

I proudly wear my two badges, the one that says DBA-IDK (Don't Bother Asking-I Don't Know) and the other that says BTO-IND (But That's OK-I Never Did). They remind me that the sum of all human advancement still doesn't come close to giving us the control of the natural world and of world events that we believed we had largely attained.

In fact, *neither* the names Planet Corona *nor* Planet Earth actually reflect the true nature of the sphere we call "home." Closest is the Hebrew word for Earth which is *"Olam."* It is closely connected to the word, *"ne'elam"* or "hidden." So much of our physical world, of our emotional and mental makeup, and of each human is unknown and, perhaps, unknowable.

Astronomers have observed the death of a star in galaxies millions of light-years distant. Yet, we have very little understanding of what transpires in the mind of a human infant. Modern medicine cures diseases that were once common and deadly. Surgery is performed *in utero* and even by remote control.

Yet, a tiny virus, Covid-19 has laid us low and eludes the combined international efforts of researchers and drug companies to find either treatment, cure, or vaccine to put this pandemic behind us.

Much is, indeed, hidden on our Olam. However, much of it is hidden in plain sight. In the story of the flight of Hagar and her son Yishmael, when the child is lying feverish with no water available for either of them, it says that Hashem opened Hagar's eyes and "she perceived a well of water" (Genesis 21:19). Many commentaries point out that it does *not* say that a well was sent, but implies that it was there all the time. But Hagar didn't see it!

Ah, the things we've noticed in the last few months that were there all the time. Our habitual perception has become unhabituated. We're used to seeing aggregates. Now, many of us have slowed our pace enough so that we can see individuals. Whether those individuals are one tree in a forest, one rose on a bush, or a single human being in a crowd.

When we were speeding through life, our view was like the blurred scenery at the side of the road as one drives on a highway. Now, we can meander and marvel, stroll and scrutinize, wander and witness, stop and see the in-plain-sight hidden glories of our Olam.

So, it was right to "leave" Planet Corona. We haven't left the pandemic behind, unfortunately. One day, a mask will be no more than a memento, a souvenir of our journey. Still, we will never be who we were before this all began. And that's good.

Very, very good!

Epilogue

When the idea to ultimately publish these letters occurred to me several months ago, the question was, when do you finish writing, end the book, and begin the process of publishing? The obvious answer: when Covid-19 is gone. Indeed, some people with whom I consulted at the time advised me that the pandemic would surely be over soon (this was in May!) and perhaps interest in the entire subject would have waned. Right.

We are now in October. No one knows when we will be able to say that the pandemic is history. I decided that 70 (letters, that is) was a good number and brought the book to a close at that point. If it were only so easy to bring the pandemic to a close.

In the 1970s there was an advertising campaign aimed at addressing the terrible pollution and littering in the US. It's known as the Crying Indian commercial and can still be viewed on YouTube. In it, a proud Native American warrior is filmed canoeing down a littered and polluted river, watching smokestacks spewing filth into the atmosphere, and standing by the side of a highway as motorists throw refuse from their cars. The camera zooms in on his chiseled and austere face and focuses on a tear rolling down his cheek.

The commercial was very powerful. I know that it made a huge impression on me at the time and must have done so on others because the Keep America Beautiful campaign that sponsored this ad was very successful. The haunting image of the weeping Native American became the centerpiece of that campaign.

Today, I have another haunting and disturbing image. It is of Hashem with a tear on His cheek watching the internecine "warfare" going on in His world. Communities against other communities. Hatred filling the media. Finger pointing on all levels. In all corners of our planet, whatever we call that planet. And yet, Hashem is the Father of *us all*.

Everywhere, parents share a fervent desire that, despite the differences among and even opposing approaches of their children, those siblings will still maintain a loving relationship. If we truly wish to consider Hashem to be our parent, we must not lose sight of what makes us all brothers and sisters.

This continues to be a time of illness, confusion, confrontation, disorientation, and loss. However, it also presents possibilities for growth, renewal, creativity, introspection, and, yes, even greater empathy for others. We can work together or pull apart.

How we respond will surely impact on our personal, communal, and global futures. Our reactions and responses are in our control. For the most part, the rest is not. Wish us luck.

A Postscript

Somewhat to my surprise I found that, upon concluding all the writing for this book, I still felt the need to continue putting thoughts into words and sending them out to friends. The following piece was written shortly before the book "went to press." Several readers liked it so much that they suggested that I include it in the book despite the fact that, for all intents and purposes, the book was finished! As it is a rather upbeat article, I agreed that its inclusion, particularly at the end, might just help leave the reader with a taste of sweetness and optimism. It served me in that way.

You can follow my further writings on my website:
www.lettersfromplanetcorona.com

November 18, 2020

Yigal

Hashem has a sense of humor. For one thing, He created us, the most ridiculous creations in His Universe. But, just at this moment, I am so grateful for the humor and joy that can come, sent straight from Hashem in the strangest ways, through the agency of the most unusual messengers.

Let me explain. The last day or two, I've been feeling rather blue. The ongoing pandemic with all its attendant difficulties, coupled with the usual ups and downs of life, now exaggerated and with compounded effects, have had their impact on me. So, I had decided to sit down today and write the letter I had been contemplating for days. It's to be about humor and emuna, and I thought that by writing concerning humor I might lighten my own mood somehow.

At times, when I am less optimistic than is beneficial, my husband will remind me of one of my upbeat letters from Planet Corona, with its optimistic spin on events, and ask me, "Why don't you read your own letters?!" As in, "Doctor, heal thyself." And, as is often the case, he is so right!

Roughly an hour ago I went down to my car to run some errands and found one tire flat! This was in addition to the flat tire that I had just a few weeks ago! Consequently, both the tire and my mood were deflated. I dialed Shagrir, the pre-paid road service that is part of our insurance plan. I was told that a representative would arrive within 2½ hours. Without any other available options, I went back into the house to wait.

After about 10 minutes, I received a call from the Shagrir road serviceman saying that he would arrive in roughly 15 minutes. I showed him to the back of the house where my car was parked and went to the trunk to haul out the spare. I heard him shouting (in Hebrew) "How are you feeling? What's doing?" Since he couldn't yet see me, I assumed he was yelling into his phone. When I came around the car, I could see he was awaiting a reply. So, I answered, "I am well, b"H."

At those words, he began to change my tire, all the while shouting out enthusiastic words of encouragement. He yelled, "Am Yisrael Chai!* Nothing can get us down! We survived the Holocaust! And we will survive Corona, too."

Then he stopped working for a minute and began to sing and dance to "Od Yishama B'Arei Yehuda,"** with his hands waving in the air. I asked his name and he said it was Yigal. I responded by introducing myself. He was probably in his early 50s, a powerfully built man with a strong and energetic voice.

He then said, "You know the Lubavitcher Rebbe would sing "U'Faratzta, U'Faratzta."*** And to illustrate, he began to sing and dance once again. At that point, I ran up the stairs and told my husband, "You really have to come down here and meet Yigal!" And he did.

Yigal didn't let up for a minute. He continued to change my tire and sing and yell out encouragement and words of emuna the whole while. As he was about to leave, I told him that I was so grateful for his words and songs. That he had totally changed my mood.

He said, "Tell everything to Hashem, to our Father, our Tatte. And don't forget to say the Birchat Hamazon [Blessings after Meals] out of a book. Also, on Friday night, sing the angels in. Not in the usual way. But with real joy and enthusiasm!"

I thanked him once again and he said, "You can call the central dispatch office and tell them that Yigal of Yerushalayim serviced your car and sang for you." I assured him that I would do so.

As soon as I went upstairs, I dialed Shagrir's central dispatch office. When a representative came on the line, I said to him, "I've just had my car serviced by Yigal of Yerushalayim. Not only did he efficiently change my tire, he sang for me and completely reversed my unhappy mood. Thank you. He deserves a 'Tza'lash' [short for Tziyun L'Shevach, a mark of commendation]." The dispatcher chuckled and thanked me.

Perhaps it's people like Yigal**** who will bring the Geula that we await longingly. Avraham had his *three* angels. Today, I had *one*. Thank you, Yigal!

---

* "The Nation of Israel lives."
** "Once Again Will Be Heard in the Cities of Judah... ["the sounds of joy and gladness"]. A chassidic song.
*** "And You Shall Spread Out Powerfully." A chassidic song.
**** Yigal (a fairly common Hebrew name) means "he will redeem"; *Ge'ula* means "the Redemption."

About the Author

CHAYA PASSOW is a graduate of Stern College in New York, majoring in English literature. She taught English at Leyada, the Hebrew University High School, an elite secondary school in Jerusalem. A sought-after lecturer and teacher of Jewish studies both in formal and informal settings, she is one of the founders of Lomdot and Melamdot, a program for advanced women's Torah learning based in Jerusalem. She has had multiple careers, including significant periods as a Weight Watchers lecturer, a small-business executive, and a teacher of Jewish subjects in elementary school in the U.S.A.

Since immigrating to Israel in 2002, she has been living her dream of residing in Jerusalem, together with her husband, Eli, and enjoying being *savta* (grandmother) to a large cohort of beautiful grandchildren.

Made in the USA
Columbia, SC
02 December 2020

26133975R00143